The Truth
(About Men)
WILL SET YOU FREE

The Truth
(About Men)
WILL SET YOU FREE

DR. PAT ALLEN

AND

DON SCHMINCKE

The New Science Behind Love and Dating

The Truth About Men Will Set You Free...but first it'll p*ss you off!
© 2009 The Dr. Pat Allen WANT® Institute
3355 Via Lido, Suite 205, Newport Beach, CA 92663

ISBN 978-0-9824808-0-9

Printed and bound in the United States of America

Third Printing — January 2011
Fourth Printing — January 2013

The WANT® Institute is a nonprofit 501(c)3 California Corporation operating for
educational, scientific and charitable purposes. The Institute is also a Federally
Registered and Approved Health Care provider, National Provider Identifier (NPI)
1912034216.

The Truth About Men Will Set You Free has been written for informational and
entertainment purposes only, and is not intended to replace or substitute for any
professional therapy, medical, or other advice.

Dedicated to H.P.
—Dr. Pat Allen

To Rowan and Nolan.
—Don Schmincke

"On Blind Date we chronicle the constant comic missteps of misinformed males struggling to score. If [men] buy this book and learn from it, we might not have a show anymore."

—Rob Dames
Exec. Producer
Blind Date

"I am in love with Dr. Pat Allen. She's my guru, she can be yours. Gotta get the book! Because no woman in this world's gonna get the guy unless they go to Dr. Pat Allen first."

—Patti Stanger
Star and Creator:
The Millionaire Matchmaker

"If there's any other expert on this planet who understands men and women as much as I do, it's Dr. Pat Allen....She has insights that everybody can benefit from."

—Dr. John Gray
Author: Men Are From Mars,
Women Are From Venus

"This book made me feel so much more generous and sympathetic towards the men in my life. I learned!! We owe it to those we love to try to better understand where they are coming from, and [The Truth About Men Will Set You Free] kept me laughing out loud all along the way. Think extended witty beer commercial with credentials and a thought-provoking ending! And prepare yourself for a wild ride and rewarding ride into the basic nature of the men in your life."

—Lynne Thompson

"Omigod, this is where I've gone completely wrong with every man I have ever met in my entire life, including my brother, father, boyfriends, and sons. It's really, really great."

—Lizzy Reese

"Dr. Pat Allen knows the answer to Freud's famous question: What do women want?…If we can learn the lessons outlined in this book, we'll all have more listening, laughter, fun, sex, love, and understanding."

—B.J. Gallagher
Author: Everything I Need To Know
I Learned From Other Women

"I have even more respect for Dr. Pat Allen for her ability to tear down those relationship walls and help people create more love and laughter in their relationships."

—Yakov Smirnoff
"Famous Russian Comedian"
and Broadway Star

"Finally some practical and useful information about us guys that gives a 'heads up' to women and some insight that will help."

—Bradley Quick
Talk Radio Show Host and
Author: Help Your Self

"Guys aren't players, they're just genetically confused. How refreshing. Every woman should read this book. We'd all save a lot of money on ice cream and Kleenex."

—Jennifer Jacobs

"A huge eye opener to the amazing way our bodies function…to actually learn about the chemical responses that make women want to nest after sex and men want to flee was fascinating. It's not personal, it's primal!…all the psychology in the world isn't going to change basic biology. This is what sex education classes should be about."

—E.E. Suranie

"Mars, shmars! This is a woman's guide to understanding. REAL men! Hurrah!"

—Melissa Garcia

FOREWORD

If you are happy, self-assured, and successfully dating fabulous men, then this book is not for you. This is for women who are still seeking, or still wanting to improve their dating experience. More specifically, women wanting something more than what dating sites and relationship books have provided so far; even if it means considering politically incorrect, but scientifically accurate, concepts.

As a high-profile therapist specializing in gender issues, Dr. Pat Allen knows something about women's challenges. Rather than trendy theories from a popular relationship book, here you will learn how to date based on ancient insights combined with hard science and backed by solid evidence. Piercing into our earthiness through a dark, twisting maze of anthropology, biochemistry, physiology, genetics and evolutionary science provides unique and fun, yet sometimes upsetting, dating methods. Discovering what affects our species, and has for millions of years, however, allows us to better understand and use the powerful differences between men and women that really define our relationships...and what happens if we ignore these differences.

This point of view is based on Dr. Pat Allen's work, as well as that of many other brilliant, respected female scientists whose contributions we note throughout the text. And while its content will surprise or even dismay you, it will give you the relationship tools you've been missing, because no one else has dared to know them, and teach them.

Table of Contents

ACKNOWLEDGEMENTS:

To all of the dedicated scientists listed in the footnotes, I offer a profound "Thank You" for the foundation of my doctoral work in Androgynous Semantic Realignment, and another grateful thank-you to the thousands of my wonderful clients who helped me to prove the validity of those techniques. To my four daughters, thank you for all your help and support through the years, and a special shout-out to all my coaches and students for eagerly wanting to learn and carry this message out into the world Also, a special thanks to B.J. Gallagher and Judith Fine-Sarchielli for their editorial expertise.

—Dr. Pat Allen

First, I want to thank Dr. Pat Allen for "seducing" me with the shocking wonders that science offers to understand the human species, and understand myself (although I've often been mistaken for a lower life form). Also, this book couldn't have emerged without the feedback from dozens of women who were brave enough to take on the task of exposing themselves to the manuscript as it was being developed. I especially appreciate the longsuffering patience of Lynne Thompson, Jennifer Jacobs, Melissa Garcia, and Jill Penaloza. I greatly appreciate the help of Renee Vincent and Jenna Glatzer for their editorial review of the early drafts, and helpful suggestions. Special thanks to Linden Gross, for her patient guidance in helping me connect with what little estrogen I have in order to tone the book for the female voice. For my first venture into writing the fictional dialogues, the coaching of June English was invaluable. Thanks to Allan and Sandy for letting me spend hours at Regi's in Federal Hill, as a safe retreat where I could craft the early stages of this work on my laptop. Our internet strategy wasn't complete without the support of social media personality Pearl Armstrong. And much thanks to D.

Michael Whelan for the terrific copyediting of this edition, and to David R. for the superb layout and new cover design.

Finally, to my family for tolerating the stressed out and often missing dad that writing a manuscript often requires. Hopefully, my kids will someday read this book when they come of age; my daughter achieving relationships more successful than me, and my son growing to become a fine gentleman.

—Don Schmincke

Introduction

> Most of us women want to find a man and be cherished,
> but we keep shooting ourselves in the foot!
> We're not to be blamed for approaching relationships the
> wrong way.
> We've never been told about the evolutionary genetics that
> makes men tick.
> So we respond to them like we respond to other women…
> but they're not women, they're **men**.
> We can't blame ourselves **or** men for what we've never
> been told.
>
> — Dr. Pat Allen

"How was that date last night?" Julie asked.

"I don't know. It was OK. I'm….."

"Uh oh. What happened? I thought that was a cool guy."

"He seemed great at first, but as the night went on, I felt like….."

"Well, there're more guys out there."

"I'm tired of being alone," Sally took a sip a of her Starbucks coffee. "I'm so frustrated. I want to find a 'right' guy, but sometimes I feel like, well, it's too much trouble."

Julie sat back in her seat. "It's never easy. I've done alright but it took work," she said.

"I know. And I am working at it! I can't tell you how many relationship books I've read. And the dating sites... they're mostly a feeding frenzy for guys, but it's something. I just can't seem to find anything that makes sense for me. I mean, I just want something that's not a constant battle for me, that sustains me, and doesn't give me a headache."

"Why is this coming up all of a sudden?" Julie asked.

"Well, yesterday we were told about the office party. It was then I realized, well,who do I bring? I can call a guy friend, but they're not serious. Then a couple girlfriends came over and started talking to me. 'You'll find somebody soon'", they said. It was kind of embarrassing."

Julie nodded her head.

"I'm successful," said Sally. "I think I'm attractive. Why am I still having problems?"

Julie sat up and leaned over the table."Maybe there's a way to approach dating differently?"

"Differently?" Sally asked.

"Yeah. Differently. Because obviously the way you've been doing it isn't working for you."

"I'm just saying that after all the books and dating sites, you're still miserable. So, maybe there's something you need to do differently."

"What exactly are you talking about?" Sally asked.

"Look. The relationship I have now isn't perfect, it's a struggle at times, but it works for me. But I had to give up what I thought I knew, in order to make some progress. I had to stop believing some things about women and men, and start accepting the truth."

"What truth?"

"Well, like you, I read a lot about dating and relationships, but I felt that some authors were trying to make money telling women what they wanted to hear versus validating their advice. I mean think about that. Millions of relationship books are sold, but how many happy couples are strolling arm-in-arm with their soul-mate, smiling and enjoying a deep, satisfying romantic relationship?"

"Ok. Good point. Despite the torrent of theories, our relationships are as dismal as ever. Just look at what we girls talk about when we're together. An unending drama. 'He dumped me. Why won't he call? He's not into me. He just wants sex. I'm not pretty enough. I'm not young enough.' But what else is there?" Sally said, appearing more frustrated.

"What if there was a validated, scientific method? I mean what if we actually knew what men want. Not what we want them to want, but what they actually want. Humans have been seeking mates for millions of years. Haven't we learned anything?" Julie laughed.

"So, how can you find this stuff out?"

"There's research now, Sally. Men aren't as inscrutable as we think they are."

"Like what?"

"I know things now. For starters, sex is genetically designed for war, not love."

"Now that's different."

Dr. Pat's "Truth": The Secret Hides In Biological Soups

For over thirty years, I've worked with thousands of women seeking a different way of finding a mate. Even today, my office fills up with singles, divorcees, housewives, executives, movie stars, politicians, artists, students, office workers, doctors, and hosts of others who feel that something is missing and want something different in their relationships. As an evolutionary psychotherapist focused on marriage and family counseling, I too wanted to understand this struggle; and spent several decades doing just that! The journey required exploring many diverse, controversial, and, at the time, politically incorrect scientific research studies, and then testing them with clients willing to work with me.

The result? Higher success rates in dating and mating.

Scientific methods provide remarkable alternative ways to design fulfilling relationships and avoid a future of serial tragedies. But to get him to fall in love with you, and even marry you, means understanding and accepting the secrets of our biological, genetic soup. Women willing to do that find the power to create more successful, meaning relationships. So, I invite you to take a journey with me to find out how to do something remarkable.

Self-Inflicted Wounds?

Before we begin, I need to issue a WARNING. This journey may require us to accept that much of the damage we women experience in disappointed relationships could be self-inflicted. I've found that:

Women tend to ignore, deny and avoid the unpleasantries of our species and how it evolved rather than use that information to get a guy into a relationship that works.

So, however unpleasant or uncomfortable this data may be for you, my experience finds that many relationship challenges diminish once a woman better understands how human genetics factor into them. But you're probably asking, "Why hasn't this information been published before?" Well, it has, for many decades, but mostly in scientific journals. Some of the data, however, became so politically incorrect that some scientists, fearing the loss of their research funding, or even their careers, admitted to suppressing their findings. This probably drove many relationship book authors away from validating their opinions with research.

Fortunately today, things are changing. A lot of this information is now leaking out into the media, and more of us are open to considering its impact on our relationships. Even so, I know this material may still appear at times "unnatural," but I encourage you to keep reading. Often I hear women say, "After I understood it better, the science ultimately made my original assumptions appear unnatural, as well as illogical!"

The Truth May Piss You Off

Evolutionary truth frees us women to select new behaviors, relieve stress and increase our success in developing a loving relationship. On the other hand, as some say, "the truth shall set you free, but first it will piss you off!" This may be true, but I find that for many of us, we at least discover new choices — and that's more powerful than being oblivious to the genetic consequences of our lives. Ironically, many of the scientific findings noted in this book come from female scientists, not males! If you're easily offended by violations of political correctness and become outraged at the scientific evidence presented here, I apologize, as that is not my intention. To be clear:

I am NOT advocating or justifying a guy's controversial and painful behavior that results in divorce, fooling around, desertion or deception in order to get laid.

I simply believe that by understanding the evolutionary source of these behaviors we can CHOOSE our actions versus being unconsciously manipulated by them.

Finally, for the curious, I've footnoted the hundreds of the scientific research publications used in this book. What you will find different about this book is that I will not only describe a guy's behaviors, but I will also explain:

- Why these behaviors occur in the first place
- How they were genetically programmed into the male DNA
- Where they are useful for species survival
- What we can do to override them biologically when we are conscious of them

No matter how hard we try to avoid biology in the quest to seek men, ignoring the science of our DNA, and his, fails to make our problems go away. But the good news is:

**Understanding your genetic instincts gives you power.
More power than you've ever had before.**

Don's POV: Time to Challenge the Status Quo

When I first met Dr. Pat Allen, her frankness and willingness to upset the status quo surprised me – exactly what I needed in an advisor for my research on applying genetics in business and leadership practices. Coincidentally she was also looking for a "male" voice to help her write this book. I was flattered, but was I qualified? Voracious dating through high school and while in rock bands, as well as living off-campus at a college fraternity in Cambridge might have provided some insights; a frat brother wrote the screenplay for *Animal House* while others took Vegas as portrayed in the movie *21*. Perhaps Dr. Pat saw more in me than I did. But what was it?

When it came to relationships, I confess I didn't see much in myself. After 25 years of expeditions, research, publishing, and developing a leadership institute with thousands of CEOs, I shamefully buried two failed marriages. Business success didn't translate into relationship success. Some women felt my "guy" perspective was that of a "pompous, self-congratulatory frat boy douche delighting in overstatement and poorly substantiated arguments." Clearly I knew a lot about growing corporations, but not a lot about growing relationships.

Dr. Pat changed all that. She invited me to learn how the genetic research we were exploring for leadership development could be applied in personal relationships. This was her world. And what she taught me changed how I saw relationships forever.

When studying Dr. Pat Allen's research, her genetic insights really DID help me understand what I was doing wrong, why I failed and how I made so many mistakes. Fortunately, she caught me soon enough to raise two absolutely wonderful and brilliant kids who say I'm the greatest dad ever (…but what do they have to compare me to?). Her scientific validation about how we guys really feel and think was refreshing and effective. Why? Well, we guys don't buy relationship books because we can't relate to them. We read things like:

Don't pursue him. If he's into you he'll ask you out, you shouldn't do anything.

You are good enough to be asked out. If

you go after him you lose the control.

Self-assurance draws a man's interest. If your attitude shows that then he will want you.

We scratch our heads. These don't ring true for us, and we can't locate scientific publications supporting these assertions. Women think they should wait? The women I know who are waiting are . . . still waiting.

Contrary to these opinions, Dr. Pat's research finds that women are not powerless. In fact, there's a LOT they can do other than wait. And they do it instinctively. My 16-year-old daughter has high self-assurance; sometimes causing stress on dad from accommodating those assurances. When getting ready with her girlfriends to go out, however, there's nothing in the makeup, hair, lipstick, and clothes that exudes self-assurance. But do these things exude power? Scientists studying female behavior in mammals now know the answer...and you will too.

Periodically I'll step in throughout this book to share a guy's point of view – as well as offer pompous, frat-boy overstatements with witless jokes; but, sadly, that's what we guys do. Hopefully, it will explain why that last guy you broke up with was really a "jerk", or why we guys can occasionally appear rather selfish, rude and one-dimensional...and those are the good points! We don't deny it. When it comes to relating to women, we know we're pathetic. We pretend to have it all together, but we suck at relationships. Just ask our ex-girlfriends, wives and mothers-in-law. Remember, we're the gender that thinks:

- Folding clothes is a waste of time.
- No phone call should exceed five-minutes.
- It's not necessary to talk or listen while watching TV.
- Beer is a breakfast food and cats are a delicacy.
- Violent movies ARE educational, and a televised sport IS art.

We can't help it. We're hardwired. But knowing why gives you new approaches for finding, getting and keeping a guy.

See you in the next chapter…

Don's right. Hardwired. Certainly, the behavior can be modified, we're not victims. But that requires understanding what's really happening; how biology drives you AND him – and it does more than either of you know. Ever wonder why you get attached to men, no matter how inappropriate the relationship may be? Or why your break-ups are so very hard to get over? Think "biochemistry." You'll soon see how evolution designed you to become chemically addicted to him, for a reason! And why you don't want to let go of him! NOTE: It's because you're actually withdrawing from an Oxytocin addiction, nature's "bonding" biochemical that's common in mammals and which we'll revisit in detail later.

Just as your biology drives you, it also drives him. A man seeks multiple women with whom to mate for a variety of reasons, but chemically that drive has a lot to do with Vasopressin, the ultimate monogamy biochemical. Secreted from the same areas of the brain as Oxytocin, he'll seek monogamy if his Vasopressin level is high enough. Conversely, he'll find it impossible to settle down if it's low. But what about when he says you're the only one in his life when he makes love to you? Since the bonding chemicals Vasopressin and Oxytocin peak in his bloodstream during ejaculation, you are his entire universe...for about seven seconds.

This book is different from my previous one *Getting to 'I Do'*. In that book, I spoke to you about what to do for yourself. Now this book explains the dynamics you face when you try to date, or work on staying a couple. So read this message of virtuous, civilized, scientific dating-mating principles that will benefit you and him. And then discuss it with him!

Will this book fix your relationships? Possibly. But it will definitely help mitigate the frustration, disappointment or pain as the deeper, real issues of your life and his finally become glaringly obvious. Discovering new choices emerging from this deeper understanding allows you to:

- Enchant a guy to want you more

  effectively.

- Be aware of why you fall in love and how

  to do it more productively.

- Avoid the battles that probably shouldn't

  be fought at all.

Ready to get him into you? Let's look at what evolution designed in your biology for relationship success, and how you can still use it today.

--- SECTION I: The Foundation ---

"Why is dating so hard for me?
Every day is another episode of 'Sex in the City'.
I feel like I succeeded in finance but failed in romance;
I cracked the "glass ceiling"
but shattered my personal life."

CHAPTER 1: Eve's Rib – How Women Create Dating Problems (*when they create men*)

"When you said to look at relationships differently, I thought you meant like the Mars/Venus stuff," Sally said. "Not all that! But what do you mean sex is war?"

"It's what's underneath our relationships," Julie smiled.

"Like some deep psychological, Freudian thing?"

"Well, somewhat. But have you ever wondered why, if we all come from the same gene pool, guys and women struggle with relating to each other so much?"

"Well, not really. I just assume it's natural and we have to cope with it."

"It is *natural*. But not in the way you're thinking."

Sally looked confused.

"It's OK. Come on. Let's go across the street to the hospital. I want to show you something." Julie got up.

Lunch was almost over, but they had time. The girls walked down the street towards Johns Hopkins Hospital.

"We're close enough to the maternity section to stop in. I've volunteered there and still kept in touch with a few friends. I always enjoyed stopping by to see the newborns."

They walked past the glass enclosure viewing area.

"The boys are with the blue blankets, the girls pink, of course," Julie said.

The two of them smiled at the babies through the window.

"OK. They're precious, but what does this have to do with dating? Other than one of these happens if you're not careful," Sally chuckled.

"The point is if a certain reaction didn't happen in their mom's womb after conception you'd see nothing but pink blankets. All the boys would be perfect baby girls,"

"What?"

Dr. Pat's "Truth": Females Make Men Different (*they didn't have a choice*)

In my earlier book *Getting To 'I Do'* I wanted to help women understand how to relate effectively with a man in order to get him to marry her. Since then a lot of new research has supported and extended those findings. In this book, however, I want to focus on the particular biological foundation – how guys evolve into becoming so different from us. Understanding this explains why we have such a hard time dating, mating, and just trying to get along with them.

Julie is right in the story above. Men are more like us early in their life. In fact, they are us! Scientists now know that when first conceived, males actually are female; the default state of a fetus. Indistinguishable from women during their first six weeks as an embryo, each embryo has unisex gonads and two sets of plumbing called Wolffian and Mullerian ducts. But if you looked real, real closely you would see a tiny difference. Males have an XY chromosome. Us? We have an XX pair. Left untouched, guys would be born female, like us; which does happen sometimes in rare medical conditions. But because of that Y chromosome, most are converted into a guy due to a very special event that occurs in their mother's womb (actually that was probably the second special event).

On a dramatic reversal of the biblical Adam's rib story, during the seventh week of gestation, the Y chromosome switches on, but only for a few hours – and man is created from woman. Scientists think this switch triggers an allergic reaction inside of us that causes a release androgen onto the fetus. This triggers a Y-chromosome sex gene that then sets off a series of genetic relays transforming him into your fondest dream or worst nightmare – a guy waiting to happen! The ensuing genetic cascade turns a guy's gonads into testicles, which then start producing a couple different male hormones, namely testosterone and the anti-Mullerian hormone; this latter hormone effectively destroys the male's Mullerian ducts. Why? So they don't become the fallopian tubes, uterus and vagina. Meanwhile his testosterone hormone protects his Wolffian ducts, which later develop into the male genitalia.

Other influences from this androgen also eliminate a guy's breasts; maintain more motor neurons in his spinal cord for the muscles attached to his penis and starts wiring his brain to be a guy's brain. Even though there is disagreement as to the mechanisms, no one argues that male and female brains are different. Further proof of this occurred recently at UCLA when scientists found brain genes that switch on in female mice embryos are less active in males and vice versa.[i]

As a female embryo without a Y-chromosome, you didn't get this androgen bath. Your process of becoming was just the opposite of a man's — destroy the Wolffian ducts while protecting the Mullerian ones. Then, without male hormones to protect your neurons for penis muscle movement, they degenerated.[3]

Guys Are First Created as Women.

This process of transformation from female to male explains how men became so different from us. Now I know some feel that revealing such radical biological differences between men and women promotes discrimination against women, but this fear is unwarranted. Scientific findings show no justification for discrimination. Dr. David Buss, evolutionary psychologist formerly at Harvard University and now at the University of Texas says, "neither sex can be considered superior or inferior to the other, any more than a bird's wings can be considered superior or inferior to a fish's fins." [ii] So, if you think emphasizing the differences between men and women is bad, you're in for a big disappointment because – *prepare yourself* – men and women are different! And I don't mean our sex organs. For starters, we have different:

- Hormone levels
- Brain wiring
- Biochemistries
- Instincts
- Smells

- Visual advantages (*especially in the color and peripheral ranges*)
- Neural activity patterns
- Heart configurations (*heart attacks are more subtle and less painful for many women*[iii])
- Eye configurations
- Finger lengths – a guy's ring finger is longer than his index finger, but women's are usually the same length. [iv] (*Go ahead and check. No one's watching*)
- Auditory advantages
- Reactions to pheromones
- Motor skills
- Brain lobe orientation

Don's POV: Denial of Biology is Useless

It was arrogant of me to think I was in control. I mean, I took enough self-help seminars. How hard could it be? But analyzing how I fell into relationships, and what drove me unconsciously, really woke me up. Argue as I might, the scientific research clearly exposed my denial.

Many of my relationship choices emerged automatically – from the genetic differences imprinted on me. Perhaps denial seemed easier because modern hype seduced me into thinking that I could make my primal instincts disappear, or be ignored. Evidence supports this. We possess the remarkable capacity to ignore the high failure rates of marriage counseling while the only thing exceeding relationship book sales is the number of failed relationships. But what do we do?

Assuming complete control, and ignoring biological influence, proves disastrous. That androgen bath in our mom's womb seriously altered our destiny. And yours![v] For example, I know we guys like to show you we're in control, but it isn't really happening. Even day-to-day interactions with you drive uncontrollable instincts. Like if we're in the office and there's a mutual attraction between us, you may want to engage us in a conversation; perhaps to find out what we do after work, our hobbies, what we like to read, where we like to hang out, our family, and friends, etc. No problem for you. But for us? OMG. As you walk up to us at the water cooler we're not thinking about any of that. Beneath that "cool" confident image honed from years of self-help training, our body's endocrine system is exploding. We're concocting an awesome hormonal cocktail as our blood pressure escalates, muscles tense, body heat increases and sweat leaks from our pores! Meanwhile, dormant brain regions (the ones that forgot to take our self-help seminars) light up, our skin cells start squandering pheromones and our eyes dilate as we lamely try to hide an out-of-control cardio-respiratory rate. Not to mention a number of changes in other parts of our anatomy.

Sadly, in relationships, our million-year-old biology wins. I remember having a trainer who was an ex-Navy Seal. Who knows what bravery this guy saw in the field, but when he had to talk to a girl he liked, he freaked. He crumbled! It was the only thing that scared him. In spite of equality of the sexes in the workplace, you already know we guys aren't equal. We're different. I mean we know what happens every time you get up to go to the bathroom together. You're talking about us! Sometimes it's because you think we're insensitive, arrogant, uncultivated, shallow, and self-centered. You're right, I admit it, but that's not the point. The point is that if you want us to want you, to love you and to commit to you, it's helpful to understand our differences. This doesn't mean complying with our different drives and instincts, we can choose to override those, but occasionally, when our biology takes over we need a little forgiveness. Our genetic drive is eternally vigilant trying to find a weakness in our defenses.

Perhaps we need to stop ignoring our biology. Our bodies will simply not allow us to leave our primal instincts behind. They never did.

Unfortunately, even though guys like Don can accept their differences, the androgen bath conversion they go through doesn't come without costs. Illnesses comprise yet another difference between our genders. Studies find that boys suffer more neurological disorders like schizophrenia, autism and dyslexia than girls.[vi] Furthermore, just as biological differences between the sexes impact everything from disease to physical features, they also impact how men and women see and relate to the world, and the people in it. Ignoring these differences hinders women in finding a guy, captivating him and getting him to commit. Not accepting evolutionary differences in our attitudes condemns us to continued frustration and arguments.

**Denying biology, denies relationships.
Instead, accept our differences
and stop trying to change each other,
...and certainly don't apologize
or feel guilty about your gender.**

Dating-Success Tips: **Understanding Him**

Undooming the relationships you'll develop after reading this book occurs when we women better understand those differences that may become annoying. After a guy evolves from being a female to becoming a male in his mother's womb, his newly acquired differences can be a challenge for the rest of his life. Some show up as minor irritations or, worse, total relationship failures. In the search for a relationship that works, it's helpful to remember that:

- Guys aren't jerks intentionally (it just comes naturally).

- If they screw up, try to forgive them.

Guys hear, see and feel differently than us, and understanding this helps produce better relationships in spite of the annoyances. Let's take a look at a few:

Why He Eats to Feel Good. You? Not So Much

After a good dinner guys feel pretty good and are usually ready to settle down to a nice cup of coffee…or other adult activities (yes, they will skip the coffee). But you? Not so much. You're thinking about whether the kids have finished their homework and are ready for bed, whether the laundry's done, whether you can call your friend to see if she's feeling better, and when you're going to get to the store to pick up a dish for tomorrow's party.

Scientists now know why. Positron emission tomography (PET) studies revealed the problem. In his research, reported in the *American Journal of Clinical Nutrition*, Angelo Del Parigi of the National Institute of Diabetes and Digestive and Kidney Diseases found that after eating, men's brains showed higher activity in the prefrontal neocortical areas for feeling satisfied, but women's showed such activity in occipital neocortex where vision is located.

What's the evolutionary advantage? When guys came back from the hunt, they needed to eat. Once full and feeling good, they could rest up for the next day. Females on the other hand needed to make sure the men were fed and adequately rested so they could catch food and kill enemies the next day, which in addition to food preparation meant the women would be handling the kids and other camp-management issues. No post-dinner lounging by the fire for them.

Some scientists think this difference in how we deal with food could also explain why women have higher rates of obesity and eating disorders than men. Guys eat, feel good, and stop. Women eat, don't feel good, and seek more food. Guys also probably don't care as much about how they look with extra weight because women want men for more than looks (more on this later).

If feeling good after eating isn't on the agenda for you, it's probably because after eating there's more to do. This sounds unfair, but remember; at least you don't have to kill things! Sure, these days men don't often need to kill animals (or bad guys) anymore, but most of you love to have a guy around when you see a spider.

Does this change when eating out? Evidence points to your feelings about eating and the satisfaction you experience afterwards shifts when you dine out. Why? Because the experience is about more than just the meal.

Females go out to dinner to nurture relationships, not as an alternative to cooking and cleaning up.

On the other hand, during dinner a guy's thoughts about moving food into his mouth are only interrupted by moments of sexual fantasy.

How He Notices Things, But You Notice People

How you both prioritize "things" versus "people" is an even more dramatic difference that requires forgiveness. You see, guys prioritize life around things. That's right, "things." You know, like "stuff." Guys actually like stuff. They spend millions on books and magazines about stuff, study how stuff works and play with computer stuff, car stuff, stereo stuff, gadget stuff, sport stuff, and hunting stuff.

Of course, we women think men are wrong when they limit their view of the world to just stuff. Yet guys think it's bizarre that we feel the world isn't about stuff, but something else — human relationships! That's why we spend millions on books and magazines written about love, romance, other people's relationships, and how to look better to other people through exercise, diet, make-up, clothes, etc. The differences between us kind of looks like this in the brain:

GUY BRAIN	FEMALE BRAIN
How stuff relates to other stuff	How people relate to other people
How to get stuff	What impact relationships have on others
How to beat someone else at getting stuff	How to fit in when relating to others
How to protect your stuff	What others think about us
How to get stuff efficiently.	How people communicate, cooperate, love and share their relationships

Researchers such as Helen Fisher, author of *Anatomy of Love*, think this brain wiring for things versus relationships makes sense evolutionarily, because a guy needs to know about "things" in order to hunt and fight better. On the other hand, females need to notice the needs of infants and other's in the community.[8] This explains a lot. A guy doesn't have to care about another guy's feelings as long as he hits his target!

This genetic difference in a guy's orientation for things versus people could be a major contributor to the fights we have about love. Women want men to tell them they love them, but guys want to "show" them instead. Ever wonder why when you ask a guy "Do you love me?" he always says:

- "Didn't I tune your car?"
- "Didn't I get you new tires?"
- "Didn't I fix the sink?"
- "Didn't I buy you jewelry?"
- "Didn't I name my boat after you?"

Guys show their love by doing, not talking.

— RULE OF DATING —

Guys use things to prove love. Girls use love to prove things.

Guys' focus on things as opposed to women's focus on people explains a lot:

- Guys can actually program home stereo, TV, and sound equipment better than women (68 percent versus 16 percent).

- 70–80 percent of guys find work (the hunt) to be the most important part of their lives, but 70–80 percent of women say it's the family (the gathering).

- Police notice in crime reports that guys are more likely to remember the make and model of the car, while females remember the suspect's hair color and clothing.

- If Barbara, Robyn, Lisa and Ellen go to lunch, they call one another

Barbara, Robyn, Lisa and Ellen. But if Jay, Allan, Mike and Bill go out for a drink, they refer to each other as Dickhead, Jerkoff, Numbskull and Useless[9]

- Guys will respect each other's stuff, while women steal each other's fashion ideas!

What Stops Him From Talking as Much as You

The fact that men don't talk as much as we do is not surprise. We've been complaining about men's lack of conversational skills for thousands of years. But now we can forgive them more easily and help diminish relationship friction by understanding the biological reason for this disparity. Recent brain scans of glucose utilization and other activity show a guy's brain is more compartmentalized. In other words, his speech function is focused in specific areas of the brain. Female speech centers, however, are distributed throughout their brain. That explains why we can talk so much...endlessly from a guy's point of view.

Is there an evolutionary advantage to this? Some scientists think so. The past ten million years, guys learned not to talk while hunting or warring because the noise scared the prey or gave away their positions. Those guys who did talk starved to death or were killed; their genetic line is now extinct. Those who survived are our ancestors.

Today a guy's centralized speech centers affect him in many ways:

- Speech defects such as stuttering are almost entirely restricted to males.

- There are three to four times as many boys as girls in remedial reading classes.

- A 1999 survey of one thousand telephone users of British phone company Telewest revealed that half of men's calls were less than five minutes, but a third of women's calls were more than fifteen minutes!

Researchers like D. McGuiness, who wrote *Sensory Biases in Cognitive Development: Male-Female Differentiation —A Bio-Cultural Perspective,* find that these communication differences occur worldwide. And there's nothing we can do about it to make each other the same. Women are more verbally fluent everywhere as discovered in studies around the world including U.S., England, Czechoslovakia and Nepal.[10]

What's our verbal edge over men? Estrogen. Studies show that we are more verbally proficient in the middle of our monthly cycle when our estrogen levels peak.[11] After menses, estrogen levels drops along with our proficiency. Still, even at our worst, we outperform males on all verbal tasks.

So, together with this new level of understanding, we can create more satisfying relationships by guys not criticizing us for talking so much and us not making them feel wrong because they're quiet.

But aren't guys good at anything? Yes, math. Although there are many brilliant female mathematicians, the ratio still goes to the guys. Research by C.P. Benbow and L.C. Stanley, seen in the article "Sex Differences in Mathematical Ability," published in the journal *Science*, found that guys performed better in higher math (not arithmetic, but the headier stuff) as evidenced in a study of 50,000 students: the highest SAT scorers were guys by a ratio of thirteen to one![12] And more research by G. C. Leder, author of *Gender Differences in Mathematics*, discovered that three out of four math PhDs are guys.[13]

Male hormones explain men's dominance in math because females who get abnormally high doses of male hormones in the womb from fetal malfunctions or drugs do much better at math than other girls. Evolutionarily this makes sense since guys needed to calculate stuff more than we did in order to hunt, fight wars and make fun toys.

Please don't interpret this as us being inferior. Remember, a fish's fins don't work well on a bird, and vice versa. I know what you're thinking, "Well, who likes math anyway? It's boring." This, of course, proves the point.

Why Guys Can't Share Emotions (so stop waiting for that to happen!)

We get very frustrated with guys because they can't share emotions easily. But, yet again, scientists now know why. Brain scans find that we recognize emotions much more quickly than they do. Researchers Dr. Raquel Gur, neuropsychiatrist at the University of Pennsylvania and her psychologist husband Ruben Gur, found that "A woman's face had to be really sad for a man to see it." This explains a lot!

- How come he didn't notice something was wrong?
- He never seems to care when I'm upset!
- All he could say is "What did I do?"

A friend of mine shared that when she and her husband bought their first house she had such buyer's remorse that she sobbed all day after the closing. They were driving separate cars and when he stopped to ask her about where she wanted to go for lunch, he didn't even notice the tears streaming down her face. Stunned, she answered him without further comment, and stared in disbelief as he just walked back to his car and drove off to lunch.

But even if guys could recognize emotions, they often can't share them for several reasons:

Reason #1 — The Brain

Male left-lobe dominance in their brain focuses guys on "thinking," while female right-lobe dominance focuses them on "feeling." Dr. Teow-Chong Sim of Sam Houston University demonstrated this recently. Because the right-side of the brain controls the left side of the body and vice-versa, he
found that women hear "emotional" words through their left ear about 6 percent better. You might let your guy know that he could have a better chance whispering "sweet nothings" to you in your left ear versus your right.

Reason #2 — Compartmentalization

Guys can't get emotional because their brains aren't wired for it. Canadian researcher Sandra Witleson found in MRI scans that emotional centers in the brains of men and women look like the picture below. As you can see, emotion in a female brain is spread everywhere:

CENTERS OF EMOTION

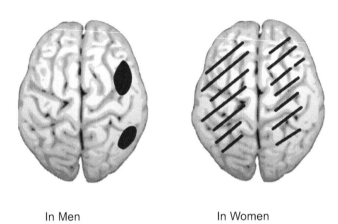

In Men   In Women

Reason #3 — Bad Chemistry

Later you will learn even more about the biochemicals Oxytocin and Serotonin, and how they help mammals to bond and share feelings. Not surprisingly, guys seem to have less of both of these than we do.

Reason #4 — Size Does **Matter**

There's also a physical reason guys can't share emotions: It's due to the neurological bridge between their right and left brain lobes called the corpus collosum. Like a high-speed data link, the thicker this bridge the higher the bandwidth between the lobes. Bigger corpus collosums allow humans to think with both hemispheres better and shift more easily between warrior and artist, thinking and feeling, masculine and feminine. The bad news is guys have smaller ones than we do! To make matters worse, new research finds there's another part of a guy's brain called the "cingulate gyrus" where emotions are located. Surprise — it's larger in us than in them.[14]

Guys don't share their feelings because they can't!

Actually they can, but by the time they squeeze emotions through their smaller corpus collosum, jumpstart a dormant cingulate gyrus, and squeeze out the last drops of Oxytocin and Serotonin, they're pretty much too exhausted to talk about their feelings.

To make matters worse, right-handed guys are more handicapped than left-handed guys and gay guys because these groups have bigger corpuses too! In fact, a Canadian study of twenty-three thousand people found that left-handed, gay guys had 39% bigger corpuses than heterosexuals! Sadly, everybody else can switch lobes faster than a hetero, right-handed guy. Right-handed guys have to work hard to shift from the logical (left) side of their brain to the emotional (right) side. Some guys are so hyper-male that they can't get off the left side. Luckily, those hyper-males die young because they're not having any fun anyway. Right-handed guys can switch, but it just takes a lot more time than women, left-handers and gay males.

So, don't get upset when a guy just answers "fine" to the question "how are you?" He thinks he's provided a perfectly sufficient answer. We should never ask a guy how he feels unless he's gay or left-handed, or we should expect to wait a couple weeks for an answer. This explains why we can think and feel while talking, but why guys get that blank look on their faces when we ask them, "How do you *feel* about…" But if we ask a guy "What do you *think* about...," they can give us an immediate answer. This causes such intense conflict that David Buss' research on newlyweds found 45% of women complain that their husbands fail to express their true feelings. And that it gets worse, not better, over time:

Year of Relationship	Percent of women who say their mate ignores their feelings	Percent of men who say that women are too moody and emotional
Dating	25%	19%
Year 1	30%	34%
Year 4	59%	49%

Why are guys so evolutionarily designed to restrict emotions? Some scientists think that not getting emotional may help them play around more sexually in order to maximize genetic success, or help them focus on other goals than relationship building. This could be true because guys find that emotional women consume far too much time and effort that could be better spent on other things important to them; things like "stuff." We, on the other hand, are more concerned about emotions because of the high risk of erring when we try to assess a guy's commitment. When we select the wrong guy, the consequences are higher for us than him!

Knowing how we're different and why nature made us that way helps heal many relationship problems and prevents a lot more. But how do we get the relationship we want? Let's find out, but not so fast. There's one more thing about gender differences you need to know BEFORE you start selecting a guy.

Sex.

CHAPTER 2: Why He's Right. It's All About Sex!

"I used to think that relationships were magical," said Sally. "I'd find that special knight and he'd carry me off into the sunset. But now you're talking to me about chromosomes!"

"This research doesn't mean you can't have a fulfilling and happy relationship, Sally. It just means that the problems we have as women are fixable if we accept the reality of what we're working with. How many lunches and late-night phone calls have you and I had consoling girlfriends. They got dumped for another lover, or found out somebody wasn't really interested?"

"You're right. None of this is new. Look at all the TV shows, movies, magazines and novels about this. I'll bet you tonight the evening news shows another celebrity or politician getting dumped, caught or divorced."

"Yet we still try to find someone."

"Why try? I mean wouldn't it be easier to just stop?" Sally shook her head.

"Sure. Yeah." Julie said with a laugh. "But we don't stop — no matter how painful it is. We're programmed to want, to lust, to find warmth in each other no matter how many failures there are. The instinct driving us to mate is too strong."

"Well, that's obvious."

"But if it's obvious, why don't we notice it? It just lurks in the dark. We hold it like data from some textbook. We never see it driving our decisions, or destroying our careers." Julie said.

"But haven't we evolved past this mating thing?" Sally asked.

Julie laughed. "Unfortunately evolution doesn't work that way. Or that fast!"

Dr. Pat's "Truth": How Love Drives You, But Sex Drives Him

Julie is right. Our bodies still operate on millions of years of programming. A successful programming, I might add, given that we're still here. This insight remains hidden to us and only reveals itself as we expose Nature's talent for being the great seducer and deceiver. Nature masks its cold sex agenda quite nicely under the modern pretense of "sophistication" — we call it romance or love. This doesn't mean we can't feel love, or have spiritual capacity for love, but research finds that underneath our civilized, sanitized, and politically correct world something else exists – Nature's genetic "prime directive". A directive secretly and unceasingly moving us toward each other, our relationship pains, disappointments and frustrations notwithstanding. And that agenda is simply to replicate the information in our cells. For gender-based species like us, that means sex. Disagree we might, but this makes perfect sense biologically.

We aren't from different planets.
We first saw each other on earth in the mud and the slime
over one hundred million years ago.

We feel we need to cover all this up with culture, religion and philosophy, however in the end Joann Ellison Rodgers, author of "Sex: A Natural History", says it best: humans are "throbbing collections of protoplasm whose energies are ever in screaming search of sex."[16] Don't expect this "screaming" to stop anytime soon. Those of us who learned to replicate survived; the rest are toast...history... gone! How many didn't make it? Scientists calculate over 99% of all species that ever lived are now extinct. We're the offspring of those who survived by successfully replicating for millennia.[17] Congratulations!

Survive we are programmed to do. That means replication of our DNA. Without that, there isn't any need for male bodies to seek female bodies. And so we will, but not without problems.

— RULE OF DATING —

Our "romantic and civilized" sophistication suppresses
nature's genetic agenda.
Humans are the only mammals
that seek to do this in their species.

Mating Ritual Collisions from Y-Chromosome Contamination

- Melanie meets the guy of her dreams. They've met for dinner a couple times. But now he's coming on too strong. She starts feeling uncomfortable. She likes him, but she's not yet ready for that next step.

- Joyce has been with Chuck for a year. At lunch, she complains to her girlfriends about the fights they're having. He wants sex too much. He's feeling rejected, she's feeling pressured.

- Stephanie sees him approach at the party. She feels excited to meet him. He delivers a bad pickup line about spending the night with him. She rolls her eyes and walks into another room.

The sex conflict is nothing new. And you do NOT have to have sex to date him, but realizing HIS agenda helps you cope with the tension and maybe even cut him some slack. Not that every guy should get some slack, but if he's salvageable it helps to understand what's going on inside his body. Evolution designed guys to see sex as the foundation of relationships, and that's why they just can't help it. For thousands of years we have complained:

"Is that all you want me for is sex?"

"Don't break your neck checking her out!"

"You're always thinking with your little head!"

And now we know why. Don't we want sex too? Yes, but eventually we also want other things, like conversation. **So the issue isn't really about sex, but the priority for it.** The ensuing tension in some strange way is nature's strategy for the genetic survival game. We are cautious — we seek to have sex with the special man who will meet our standards (which are also set by genetic evolution for offspring protection), while guys seek the one woman who will...well, just say "yes." I know that some of us get very upset when they hear that guys just want to get laid, but remember, denying it doesn't make it go away. Let's see how we can work with it versus getting hurt by it.

Why the Male Sex Fixation: Snails and Puppy Dog Tails . . . with Testosterone

What's the culprit triggering man's high sexual fixation? A nasty little molecule called Testosterone. A very ancient hormone, the "Big T" turns on the neural pathways for lust and the ones for aggression. Testosterone has been wreaking havoc on male biology for millions of years and begins its agenda at puberty. That's when testosterone makes sure guys only think about one thing — sex.

Testosterone forces men to look at women. It's nature's most common response. If men don't look at women, they're either gay or something's wrong. But we probably won't ever say, "Honey, you didn't even glance at that pretty girl walking by? Is everything OK?" And that's the paradox of our species. Recently, many published studies reveal testosterone's impact on a guy's sex drive and aggressive lifestyle.[20] For example:

- Asian men have the least amount of sex, a finding consistent with their lower level of testosterone… and lower incarceration rates.

- Guys with nine-to-five jobs have less sex than guys who work sixty-plus hours per week (another testosterone signal).

More research reveals how testosterone drives men to sex by observing sexual desire rates dropping just as testosterone rates drop as men get older. Even though everyone said they were happy with their sex life, a study of couples in Australia in 1997–1998 showed sex frequency to be as follows:

Frequency of Sex per Year	Age
144	20
112	30
78	40
63	50
61	60

These are just averages, of course, because some guys are still virgins in their twenties while others hump like rabbits until they're sixty, but overall men lose testosterone's aggression and havoc as they age.

Curiously, this loss of testosterone's influence accelerates once guys mate for life. Some research suggests that this explains why men tend to lose their edge for professional success shortly after marriage, while unmarried men seem to keep achieving success well into their fifties and sixties.[19] Professional success reemerging after a divorce further supports this effect – testosterone increasing once again after the marriage is over.

Not surprisingly, testosterone havoc hurts us in relationships; causing men to want polygamy, to want more than one wife, and to want sex often and with many females. It's the main culprit challenging monogamy and making us angry as it promotes one-night stands, which Dr. Theresa Crenshaw says is as close to being alone as possible with another person.

But does testosterone affect us too? Yes, but we have a more dominant molecule.

What's Your Hormone? Sugar and Spice and Everything Nice

Estrogen is our magic. This hormone causes us to behave in ways men find exciting. Our estrogen-driven behavior makes men want to be sexually aggressive and, interestingly, to show off in order to get our attention. Estrogen turns us into Marilyn Monroe — warm and seductive — by developing our breasts, our smell and our receptivity to sex. It makes us sexual magnets for men, especially when estrogen levels peak in our twenties, or we undergo estrogen replacement therapy later in life. Even though our estrogen makes us willing and available, however, it doesn't necessarily inspire us to act. That's HIS job. Our job is to influence his action.

As part of our replication design, estrogen makes us want sex too, but contrary to men (who want it for its own merit), we women want it for approval and to feel valued.

— RULE OF DATING —

Estrogen makes you want sex not for an orgasm, but so that a guy will approve of you.

This does not diminish us as women. Seeking approval is important. In a quirky way, nature gives us power to manipulate males for approval so we get what we want – resources and protection for newborn children.

Do guys have estrogen too? Yes, but there's so little of it, that it won't affect them until their testosterone level drops as they get older, which is why we actually find older guys to be nicer guys. Some feel this is why young women and old men bond so well. We may get judgmental when we see a sixty-year-old male with a thirty-year-old wife, even if you don't live in Hollywood, but this loss of testosterone may explain it.

Conversely, as we women get older our estrogen goes down and we begin reacting to our levels of progesterone. Guess what we end up doing? Being as polygamous as young men. In fact, a guy's sexual performance level at nineteen years old is compatible with a woman in her later thirties to early forties. Meanwhile, a guy's sex drive in his forties is compatible with a woman in her early twenties. That's why some women feel "used" for sex by their husbands when they're in their twenties and thirties and some husbands feel like they're being demanded to perform sexually when their wife reaches her forties.

Don's POV: Blame Testosterone

Sometimes I try to find a great guy movie I can watch with my 12-year-old son. It's bonding time! But with many movies rated 'R', our selection quickly becomes somewhat limited. Yet I have to remind myself that this isn't a new problem in our society. Sex appears more prevalent now because of the media explosion — music videos, television series, magazines, web porn, shock-jocks, etc. — but it's simply not true. Sexual priority has always been there, even when TV showed Ozzie & Harriet or Dick & Laura sleeping in separate beds. The media just magnifies and overemphasizes sex today.

New archaeological evidence shows that humans were just as engaged in sexual activity in history as they are now. Substantial knowledge and practice of sex dates back 300,000 years and included various forms of:

- Prostitution
- Brothels
- Pornography
- Fetishes
- Transvestitism
- Sadomasochism
- Autoerotic asphyxia[22]

During historical research in Italy a couple years ago, we visited Pompeii; a dream of mine. Dramatically preserved antiquities in a city devastated by pyroclastic volcanic flows. Yet, the only excavated building with a very long line was…the brothel. Like many cities, phallic symbols in the cobblestones pointed to this main event – the house of sex. With instructional "menus" still preserved on the walls depicting the selections of the day, we can assume sexual prevalence occurred long before high-bandwidth media. These sexual practices over thousands of years don't make sex "dirty" (Woody Allen said it's dirty "only if it's done right"), but simply reveals that genetic replication is what human biology intends from these acts, and it's all inherited in our genetic code. If you date a guy thinking this is a new problem, then you'll miss opportunities to utilize better strategies for more effective dating.

The priority for sex continues to drive guys so powerfully that we do stupid things. Want proof? Watch the news tonight. Will it be a politician, preacher, or celebrity getting caught with their pants down? And those are just the ones that got in the news! But this drive also causes us to do good things. We'll even consider acting politically correct and sensitive, like a gentleman. Sometimes we'll even sign legal documents to give you half our stuff, even when statistically you will get half our stuff!!!

Science doesn't justify testosterone-driven behavior, but EXPLAINS it. No matter how sensitive you think guys are, our biology isn't buying it. We left that a long time ago, after the androgen bath when testosterone took control of our body and we developed:

• Facial hair
• Acne
• Voice cracking
• Broadening shoulders
• Narrowing of hips
• Leanness of muscles
• Body odor
• Sperm
• Lots of sperm
• Lots of sperm wanting release
• Lots of sperm wanting release often
• Did I mention lots of sperm?

Yes, awkward. Guy humor tends to make some of us angry, others uncomfortable, and still others feeling pity for them (even though I did chuckle at the last one). But sadly, it's not going to change anytime soon. So now let's understand why.

Why He **Won't** Change Anytime Soon

Nature doesn't have a conscience. It's just a dance. A dance to see whose genetic data wins. Because we were born into this dance millions of years after it started, we're pretty well designed to win. That's why, unfortunately, his behavior and sexual fixation won't change. It's not a culturally induced phenomenon from poor upbringing (that would be easier to fix). No. Evolution specifically designed men to preoccupy themselves with sex. This explains why men relentlessly resist us as we try to change their sexual priority regardless of the risks they will undertake.

But why can't women prevent a guy's selfish sexual priority from overtaking his career, reputation and family stability? Well, it's embedded in his Y-chromosome. Evolution made sure that his selfish sexual obsession remains unchangeable for one reason: Genetic Success. You already noticed this. Ever wonder why guys pursue inappropriate sexual encounters with secretaries, neighbors or somebody else's wife when many of these encounters result in career suicide, financial losses or, tragically, death? Chances are you've noticed this on today's news, or have a girlfriend who personally encountered such indiscretions.

Scientists think selfish genetic strategies are the best for transferring DNA information into the future for ANY species. But we women don't want to be a victim to man's creative seminal energy. **The opportunity is realizing that the Darwinian Y–chromosome he carries is the mutable, flexible evolutionary link to God's creativity.** It does not reside in Matter, Mater or Mother. And even though we hate being "Eve", with the also-ran designation by nature, we have more power in the creation of a "gentleman."

We must be cautious, however. If we try to turn him into us, it results in distress and cosmetic "boys" who can't (1) Control, (2) Conquer, or (3) Compete. Nature maintains control by continuing to punish "wannabe" men, and the women who make them that way. But if we take a different route, we can achieve much more success. Instead of trying to find or create that "girly-man" (and I know we've been told that's the way they should be), why not accept what Nature maintains anyway? I run into a lot of women who don't agree that we can't eliminate nature's influences. If that's you, please keep reading. You have nothing to lose, and a lifetime of relationships to gain.

Before continuing, let's reemphasize our earlier points:

1. Those who didn't seek sex as the foundation of relationships are now extinct. Awareness of this helps you better date, mate and love. Ignoring it doesn't create a better future.

2. Accepting his sexual drive versus trying to change it doesn't mean that you need to have sex with him, but ignoring this drive doesn't help either.

3. Primitive relationships were easier, only requiring simple gear — an erection and a female. But today the game has dramatically changed. The bad news is…our bodies haven't. Every day our ancient biological machines wake up in modern society, their designs for genetic conquest causing endless conflicts between men and women. Ignoring this "old body in a new world" condition continues to ruin relationships until we find out a way to harness it.

Life is a sexually transmitted disease with a 100% mortality rate (that can be produced by unskilled labor).

Dating Success Tips: Forgiving Him

You'll soon learn how to get into a relationship in the next section, but let's take a moment to prepare you ahead of time for that journey. A couple of tips may come in handy:

Why He Misinterprets Your Sexual Advances

If sex is a common agenda, albeit with different gender priorities, why do we sometimes get turned off by how a guy approaches us? Biochemistry helps us understand. You see, sometimes a guy's sexual advances may be from a misinterpretation resulting from nervousness or unconscious instincts. Knowing this helps us from inappropriately dismissing a guy too quickly; giving us a more powerful choice in selecting or rejecting a man.

Theresa Crenshaw's research published in *The Alchemy of Love and Lust* finds that the problem may be that the typical man gets confused about what WE want. That's because nature designed us with more than one degree of lust.[23] Knowing which hormones drive our lust explains why we react the way we do to a guy's approach. Some signals are obvious. If he pats us on the butt and we slap him, then that's probably a no. But if we respond instead by grabbing him in an unmentionable area, that's probably a yes.

However, more complex situations need to be assessed here:

— RULE OF DATING —

Guys always get mixed signals about a woman's intentions. Female lust styles can be general or genital, involve orgasm, penetration, masturbation or touch, and range from intimacy to don't-even-want-to-know-your-name sex.

Is it any wonder that guys get confused when trying to mate with us? Lots of conflict and missed opportunities can be avoided if a guy could identify our degree of lust. They think we women only have one degree of lust, but in reality, we have four. Recognizing which one we're in gives us an opportunity to clarify it for him. Why? Because he's not that smart, he's going to be clueless. Here are our lust states:[24]

Active (aggressive):

This is where OUR progesterone drives us — we pursue him! Guys love this one. In fact, just like guys, women in this state masturbate more frequently, even if a sexual partner is readily available. This is when we are most like a guy, but that's as far as the similarity goes...and why most guys get so confused with this type of woman.

Receptive (Passive):

This is where our estrogen drives us. We enjoy and welcome sex as he pursues us; and we are very receptive to his approach and easy to arouse. Surprisingly, orgasm is incidental to us in this style. Guys also like this state.

Proceptive (seductive):

This is where we become the "sex kitten," the seducer. Estrogen, Oxytocin, Progesterone and a sprinkle of LHRH (you'll learn about these later) create a powerful bio-chemical brew inside us that produces an intense lordosis response — the arching of the back and thrusting of the buttocks outwards. Also, Oxytocin levels ensure our skin sensitivity is high with a special intensity in the genital and breast area. Yes, as you probably already guessed, guys really like this one too.

Aversive (no lust):

When we lack lust, Vasopressin is driving the agenda, along with a little Prolactin, Serotonin and Progesterone in the hormonal soup; not a nice combination for a guy to be around. Our nervous system inhibits arousal, particularly in the genital area, and short circuits uterine contractions thereby blunting any orgasmic response in us. As you probably guessed by now, guys don't like this one.

So, we are complicated and require a lot of observation and maintenance, Guys? Well, they're a bit simpler when it comes to lust. Men have only one degree:

Active (aggressive):
Guys pursue sex, with or without a woman.
It doesn't matter.

The key tip for us to remember here is that when a guy misinterprets our mode of operation, it can make him appear sexually aggressive. This doesn't mean some guys aren't aggressive naturally, some are and this section won't help them, but many times a guy's sexual aggression stems from misinterpreting our advances. This is scientifically accurate. A couple of research studies published in the *Journal of Personality and Social Psychology* by Dr. Martie G. Haselton and Dr. David M. Buss show that a guy thinks we are being sexy, seductive and coming on to him about TWICE as many times as we actually are.[25] So be careful. Ironically, the same research shows that he's less bothered if we are sexually aggressive towards him!

— RULE OF DATING —

The female sex drive hasn't changed for thousands of years.
Only the freedom to speak and media-hype has increased.
Erroneously, so has a guy's expectations.

So guys assume we want the same behavior that they want! Contrary to what they feel, however, we find sexual aggression highly uncomfortable and psychologically painful. This behavioral difference between a man and a woman is also an evolutionary design. For millions of years, it's been more costly for a guy to miss a reproductive opportunity than to look like a jerk, so he takes a shot even if it makes him appear too aggressive. We women, on the other hand, suffer more consequences from abandonment with a child, so nature gave skeptical women a better genetic survival rate. This pattern explains the confusion we've been experiencing in an era where the feminist movement frees us up to talk about our sexuality and behave more similarly to men. The problem increases as the media produces a proliferation of magazines, books and movies on the hyper-sexed female. **Unfortunately, high-sexual assertiveness represents less than one percent of all women.** Still, sex remains the best way to attract a guy, whether you intend to have sex with him or not.

Forgive Stupidity

Just like lower primates, our female DNA makes us feel the need to seek out a high-testosterone male, the alpha male, the dominant leader, the muscle-bound brute who could protect us and the kids while killing big food; a necessary condition for us to replicate our genes successfully. Why do you think in some countries powerful men produce thousands of illegitimate children? This is not a good thing, but the problem is more than being seduced into having illegitimate children. High-testosterone guys can be a bit self-centered at best and violent at worst. Today, modern civilization categorizes this brute today as a temperamental monster with high-blood pressure, explosive tantrums, wandering eyes, no hair, no commitment, and an invitation to appear on the Jerry Springer Show.

Guys, however, unconsciously and instinctively know we are genetically programmed to seek high-testosterone males. This explains why testosterone makes them do stupid things to impress us. Ever notice how a guy will embarrass himself by committing a risky or extreme or inappropriate act to impress a girl? So, be aware that a lot if this is because they want you to notice, and if you get a chance, try to stop them from killing themselves.

Give Him Space: Distance Yourself When Appropriate

Paradoxically, testosterone wants to mate, and also be alone. We have a hard time with this one because we're biologically designed to be group-oriented, a necessary trait for the tribal community and social development of children. Guys, on the other hand, had to hunt and fight the bad guys, so they needed quiet and isolation to maneuver and be stealthy. Combine these factors in a relationship and it's a train wreck waiting to happen:

- Women want inclusion, guys want to be alone.
- Women want connectedness, guys want to be alone.
- Women want attachment, guys want to be alone.[21]

This explains the conflict we have when we want to satisfy him by being close to him, but he wants to be alone! His biological design for space, privacy and autonomy is why guys become irritable. A local talk show phoned a bunch of guys on Father's Day to see what they wanted as a gift. Their response validated the genetic situation we're discussing. The main responses were classic:

- "To have her be quiet."
- "To have her just leave me alone for the day!"

Does this mean guys do not want to be around us? Of course not! But testosterone is raw, nasty and as "politically incorrect" as you can get. It does want us around, but just long enough for — you guessed it — sex. Higher order brain functions mask this hormonal desire under the guise of "romance."

— RULE OF DATING —

Women feel that guys evade them. Guys feel that women invade them.

--- SECTION II: Getting A Date ---

CHAPTER 3: Dating Phase I - Detection

"OK. So women created man to be different and now sex is the major driver. Great. But, Julie, how do I use this to date differently?"

"Well, there are three phases."

"Phases? What about romance? Or love?" Sally protested.

"Well, do you want more platitudes, or do you want to know what works?"

"OK," Sally winced.

"Look, there's stuff you've got to know. It seems unromantic, but that will come later. Do you want to find a better way to get a guy or not?"

"Of course."

"Then listen," Julie whispered. "The secret phases are detection, then enchantment, then captivation."

"What a minute. Slow down. What are you talking about?"

"Let's start with the first phase, detection; getting a guy to notice you. You could be at a party or at work. If you don't get noticed, you don't get dates."

"How do I do that?"

"Trigger his sexual focus so you DO get noticed."

"What? You want me to walk in naked?"

Julie laughed. "Not exactly. It's simpler. Getting noticed means just triggering his DNA program for the unfamiliar."

"The unfamiliar?"

"Yes. You show up on his radar more if you're an unfamiliar female."

"Does this mean I have to hang out with strangers?"

"Sometimes, or you could change *you*."

Dr. Pat's "Truth": How to Get Him to Notice You

Julie is correct. Manipulating guys to notice you is not culturally unique. Multiple scientific studies find similar "attraction" methods between gender-based species everywhere, using same patterns in all countries. Not surprisingly, those same studies also find that we women are using these techniques already, just unconsciously. What I want to do with you here is make them conscious so you can better attract a guy (detection), then get him to want you (enchantment) and then capture him into a relationship (captivation).

As a psychotherapist, women come into my office trying to "fix" him, and make him more like them. But the truth is that until they accept how a guy is biologically, they aren't going to "fix" anything. If you want to catch a man, accepting him at this mammalian level will give you more ways to get him interested in you. Later when he gets serious about love, he'll be interested in your virtue, intelligence and how much you love yourself. But if you're just starting to date him that isn't going to happen yet!

Today you are just trying to get a date or keep the one you got so that later you can start, hopefully, a longer-term relationship. Until then, sexual attraction is the initial game. Use it. You don't have to have sex, but use the influence. Your hit rate increases significantly with even the most respecting, God-fearing man if you use sexual attraction as part of your strategy to captivate him. Remember, you don't have to have sex with him, but you want to use this trigger to attract and capture him.

With a guy checking out dozens of women a day, it seems a little difficult to show up as the "one." So how do we increase the odds of him noticing us? Fortunately researchers such as David Barash and Judith Eve Lipton, authors of "The Myth of Monogamy: Fidelity and Infidelity in Animals and People", found a solution. They discovered something interesting in our mammal cousins that also applies to humans. Males in species such as the Japanese macaques, Red Howler monkeys, and humans, notice and respond best to females with whom they are NOT acquainted with or familiar.[27]

Don's POV: Why Guys Want Strangers

Dr. Pat's right. Unconsciously at the cellular level, we are selfish. Our biology's interest for maximizing sperm distribution increases the probability of our genetic information surviving into the future. That's the gene's only interest. Not survival of the species, but survival of the "information" in the species. That information is DNA. So, nature makes sure that:

Guys are always on alert for newly targeted eggs — strangers in the mist.

But you're probably wondering why don't we get as excited with familiar females. Some scientists think male avoidance of familiar females may be a necessary genetic program to avoid inbreeding, a bad thing genetically and the reason that brothers and sisters don't generally mate or marry. Nature finds inbreeding distasteful because mating with someone too similar to your genetic code creates offspring with pathological problems.

But does inbreeding resistance really make you less attractive to us if we're already with you? As a guy, I'd have to agree. I always seemed to respond that way when I was dating, but that's just my observation. What does the research say? Studies suggest that evolution made inbreeding avoidance so effective that in her study of 35 gorilla bands over a period of 18 years, anthropologist Diane Fossey found only one occasion where a silverback mated with his daughter, and the infant was immediately killed by family members.[28]

But what about humans? More research exists here as well. For example, several studies of Israeli kibbutzims provide the most remarkable test of our natural tendencies to avoid inbreeding. Raised communally with common living, sleeping and bathing quarters, kibbutzim children play at sex with games of kissing, hugging and even touching one another's genitals.[29] But researchers noticed by the age of one year, these children became shy and tense with the opposite sex, and by age 15 they bonded simply as brothers and sisters. Even though they were free to copulate and marry, they almost never did within their peer group.

Another study by Joseph Shepher of kibbutzim marriages — 2,769 of them — found only thirteen that occurred between peers, but in each of them one mate had entered the communal group after the age of six! All of whom were raised since birth had no marriages and no sexual activity within the group. Further investigations by Melford Spiro found that no one even engaged in sexual intercourse with another member from the same group. (Quite a lot of restraint for several thousand teenagers with ample opportunity for sex!)

Other communities show the same need for unfamiliar mates. Research by Arthur Wolf, Stanford University anthropologist, chronicled in *Current Anthropology* reveals that in Taiwan "minor" marriages — arranged marriages among siblings of which one sibling was adopted — partners reported few erotic feelings for each other and produced 30-40% fewer offspring.[30] Clearly there is a critical period in childhood where individuals lose forever all sexual desire for those they see regularly.[31]

Biologically, rarely do "childhood sweethearts" occur. After talking to a number of women as we developed this book, however, I found that you know this to be true anyway. Somehow you subconsciously know that the best time to get noticed by a man is when you first appear as a stranger, or when you've been away and then come back with a new look. Could this have created the "makeover" industry? Not sure, but how many romance dramas depict a guy's fantasy for that dark, mysterious woman who walks into his life? You know the scene — late night, smoky and dark office: A lonely private detective gets a knock on the door and finds a sexy, knockout "broad" desperately needing his help. He knows he can save her, but he doesn't show how much he wants her. Is she secretly using him? Guys love this stuff!

Finally, this attraction for strangers also drives you! Ever notice your higher arousal when you meet a guy who's new to the group? Or what about the common female fantasy for the "tall, dark stranger," the "drifter," the "new guy on the block?" Your biology makes this sexual attraction necessary so that you have ample opportunity to integrate your egg with DNA that's new and different from your familiar group. A politically incorrect thing to say, but it is scientifically accurate.

Now let's get back to Dr. Pat . . .

Applying all this cold, genetic mammalian research to improving our relationships can feel depressing. I've had clients ask, "How can the deep romance, companionship and intimate cherishing I'm seeking be reduced to such a coarse, earthy sexual state?" I know it's tough to accept how mammalian mating instincts most effectively help us get the guy we want, but please remember that we aren't proposing a philosophical argument here. We're just presenting scientific data. Avoiding this information could be what's been missing in your dating experience. Ladies, our biology is more than adequately designed to use sex in order to get a male. So ignore political correctness, women's liberation and all the modern cultural norms we've learned. Instead, let's step back a million years and use what God gave us — a female body more than capably equipped to find and attract a man. It may at first appear offensive, but accepting opens new and exciting ways to approach chronic dating problems and maybe even lead a guy into a successful, monogamous relationship. The good news is if you still feel resistant, that's natural. Just suspend your judgments long enough to let yourself be open to different information. Believe me, the thousands of women I've worked with over decades discovered more ways to attract guys, and find a satisfying relationship. You will too!

Please note: Anything about this you find repulsive may have more to do with your culturally induced experiences, not your biology. Your biology doesn't care about cultural norms and neither does his. So if you want to spark his interest, remember biology is the only thing he's listening to.

— RULE OF DATING —

Accepting his sexual focus versus trying to change or ignore it offers more effective ways to find and keep him in a committed relationship.

Dating Success Tips: How To Appear Unfamiliar

Become a Stranger

Showing up in his environment as "new" or "different" is our best move for getting his attention. A man's primal need for the unfamiliar female gives us quite an advantage when dating. Even if we feel that we're not as unattractive as other women are, we have a better shot at getting noticed if we're "new" to the group. So the first thing to do is check out the group or social circle you are in now. How long have you been there? Are you already too familiar to the guys there? If you're no longer seen as new or different, take some action to change that. Ideas include:

1. Find a new job or position.
2. Make an effort to find new friends at work or school who are apart from the typical group you hang with.
3. Relocate to a new residence.
4. Show up at different pubs or restaurants on the other side of town.
5. Seek new social groups.
6. Try different hobbies, arts, spiritual pursuits, community associations, charities, etc.
7. Take weekend trips to other cities to hang out.

Leave and Come Back

I've found success with many clients who used this "unfamiliar female" strategy within their current social groups. Essentially chose to either:

1. Take a break from the current group for a few months and then return.

2. Consider a makeover.

Either way, the trigger effect on his nature occurs.

Once you find being a stranger to the group places you as the fresh female on his radar, you're now in a position to get him to want you. And if you think getting his attention using biology is manipulative, wait until you see how we get him to want you. That requires another set of genetic triggers.

CHAPTER 4: Dating Phase II - Enchantment

Julie and Sally met two weeks later at their favorite bistro. After ordering some drinks, Sally opened the conversation:

"I tried a couple of your ideas this week."

"Great! What happened?"

"Well, you know that professional networking group you wanted me to check out?" Sally took a sip of her glass of wine. "I did. And then I went to a baseball game."

"You hate baseball!"

"I know. I know. But someone at the office invited me to meet her husband and his friends at a game. A lot of them were single, so I went."

"What happened?"

"I noticed looks. Different than when I'm with regular friends. It was kind of fun."

"Well you don't have to abandon your friends."

"I know. But I'm seeing my hairdresser next week for a change there too. And I want you to introduce me to that fashion consultant you've been using."

"Sure. OK. This sounds like progress."

"But I'm anxious to know about the next Phase. What do I do after I get *detected?*"

"Well, you have to get him to want you."

"Sounds good. And how?"

"Enchant him!"

Sally laughed. "How? Do I sprinkle fairy dust or something?"

"No, but if you have some, use it," Julie smiled. She removed the olive from her drink and deposited it on her plate. "What I mean is you have to stimulate his sex organ!"

Sally put her fingers over her eyes then glanced between them to see if anyone was paying attention. "Be serious."

"Calm down. It's not what you think," Julie looked vaguely mischievous.

"Well, what 'organ' are you talking about?"

"I'll give you a hint. It starts with the letter 'P', is surrounded by hair and dilates to several times its normal size when properly stimulated," Julie smirked.

"That's what I thought you meant." She pointed to her lap.

"No. You have a dirty mind, and will forever be disappointed!"

"Huh?"

"It's his *pupil*, of course!"

Sally shook her head, "OK, you got me. So how do I stimulate that?"

Dr. Pat's "Truth": How To Get Him To Want You

Stimulate His Sex Organ (It's not what you think)

A guy's sex organ is not in his pants. It's in his eyes. You see, a man's visual system ceaselessly searches for and automatically detects female shapes anywhere. His brain's design makes it so. When it detects a female shape, a concoction of neuropeptides and other biochemicals surge into his bloodstream thereby initiating a rapid sexual response in his body. Nature programmed this optical/sexual system so effectively that we don't even have to say anything — female nudity alone drives his erections whether they are real, pictured or imagined!

Nature made his visual system THE main trigger for sexual stimulation, superior even to ours in its capacity for sexual arousal. His optical gear is programmed to pick a female out of a crowd anywhere, whether he wants to or not. Talk about radar! Among studies on his optical sex system, research from David Buss, author of *The Dangerous Passion*, and B.J. Ellis and D. Symons, as published in the *Journal of Sex Research,* validates male optical versus emotional sexual stimulation:

	Guys	Fema
Focus on visuals rather than feelings during sexual fantasies	81%	43%
Focus on feelings during actual sex[32]	19%	57%
Want to have sex with the lights on[33]	76%	36%

If you need more evidence, investigate the article "Influence of Popular Erotica on Judgments of Strangers and Mates" published in the *Journal of Experimental Social Psychology.* Psychologists Douglas Kenrick, Sara Gutierres and Laurie Goldberg found that guys had less "love" for their mate when shown Playboy pictures. Playgirl pictures, however, did not have that effect on women.[34]

This visual sex organ explains why pornographic images have such an effect on men. It also explains why he never cares about what career we have, what our interests are, whether we're self-assured, where we're from, who we know or what our values are. All he cares about is how we look! And, yes, we already know how he wants us to look – naked. It's all in his biology and there's nothing we can do to change it.

So Where Is Our Sex Organ?

As women, our ears, not our eyes, contain our secret for sexual arousal. Think about it. What happens when he gently leans over, slowly moves his lips across your cheek, then to your ear and whispers his most intimate feelings for you, how he has so longed to touch you, and so desperately wants you in his life? Your eyes close in ecstasy. You see, for us, the emotional dimension of the relationship stimulates us... and verbal expression of it, not a photo, works best.

We see this often in our sexual media. Men seek strip joints or pornography, while we women stack up on romance novels, women's porn. This explains why sales of pornographic pictures and films to women are just as low as the sales of romance novels to men. And don't deny it. "50 Shades" didn't become a bestseller from guys buying it!

Once, a client asked me, "But what about all those nude male calendars that get sold, don't women get aroused by those visuals?" Good question. But research shows that we don't. These types of calendars are bought by:

- Female teenagers who just want a picture of their favorite star
- Older women who bought it as a joke for a friend
- Gay males.

So, if a guy wants to get us excited, he doesn't show us a naked picture (most of us would start laughing). Instead, he starts to talk to us about things like commitment, time with us, intimacy and nonsexual touching. But a naked picture of us — or almost any other semi-attractive woman — is all HE needs to get excited.

Don's POV: The Eyes Have It

How many times do we hear guys complaining about how long it takes a woman to get ready to go out? Pointless to argue. It's instinctive. Contrary to what the experts say, when a guy meets you, his visual stimulation of you surpasses any interest in your conversation. Your self-assurance doesn't draw his interest, your self-portrayal does — how you look! You know this. Those hours getting your hair, makeup, and dress "ready" are for visual effect. Your date may be interested in your deeper values later, when marriage enters the picture, but his initial response is visual (you're not expecting a marriage proposal yet – the design of that journey is a whole other book). Right now the game is about dating, attracting and getting a guy to want you. The best way to get him to want you is activate his sex organ!

Even though the evidence is clear, accepting men's visual stimulation becomes the toughest part for some women to accept. Look at the anger in the media every day. For example, remember the Miller Lite's "Catfight" commercial with wrestling females. Major upset with women! USA Today quoted one woman as saying, "Every time I see it I cringe. It's explicit. It's degrading. It has no real message, except all men are idiots and all they think about are girls mud wrestling."[35] But it sold well with guys. Women got angry, guys loved it. That's a clue.

Another example was a few years back when a female newscaster interviewed a female star of a movie about strippers. She asked the actress whether she felt stripping supported perversion or provided a safe haven for its expression and appreciation. The problem was that these two women were pondering a question without the required optical/brain sex capacity to understand, let alone answer it. Remember that men will always be stimulated by visuals of nude females regardless of perversions, whether it's on the street or in a safe haven, and precisely because nature made sure that they would! Evolution designed men this way so they'd mate efficiently.

If you still don't believe any of this, look around you. If a naked girl walks past a bunch of guys, they will all get sexually aroused. But if a naked guy walks past a bunch of girls, they start laughing. When a woman puts on a little weight and feels her guy might be losing interest, or may even be cheating on her, the experts say to dump him. What? Who wrote this? Have they read any scientific journals over the past 50 years? They NEVER say to use the genetic agenda. They never mention that while you want to "hear" nice things from him, he just might want to "see" nice things from you. Many women lose weight when dating, but gain it after marriage. They call it their "marriage weight"; only seeking it again when divorced. But there's a reason women do this instinctively. One popular female website says: *"Don't ask him if you are gaining weight. Avoid self-put-downs like, 'I'm getting fat.' Feeling confident about yourself makes you sexy."* But think about that advice for a moment. Wouldn't it be easier to keep him by losing weight BEFORE he leaves? This is a tough topic to swallow. But timely. Obesity in the U.S. and other countries has reached epidemic levels.

Regardless, all women can improve visual stimulation.

Don's POV may sound raw, but clearly visual stimulation is unique to guys, and can be so intense that it even permeates his spiritual enlightenment. Buddha said: *The pleasure and joy that arise in dependence on the eye: this is the gratification in the eye. That the eye is impermanent, suffering and subject to change: this is the danger in the eye. The removal and abandonment of desire and lust from the eye: this is the escape from the eye.*[36]

His visual trigger for nudity is a tough concept for us to accept. Many books dance around this issue or avoid it all together. But genetic programming doesn't go away because it's ignored, try as we must. An article titled "But Do Girls Want To Be Fancied By Men Behaving Badly?"[37] was written by a woman who referenced a Playboy study of the top 100 sexiest stars. She concluded that guys, being so predictable, only go after big-breasted blondes with shapely figures. She ended the article with,

"I don't think we want men like that to find us sexy, thanks all the same." The only problem is her dating life must be miserable. I know. My office is full of women like that.

The good news comes from clients who follow the advice we're giving you here. Even if you're an average woman who is not drop-dead gorgeous, or candidate for trophy wife, this research works dramatically when applied. Think about those "makeover" shows where they take a plain-looking girl into the back room and she comes out looking gorgeous. Maybe not movie star sexy, but certainly appealing enough to turn a man's head. That's all you need to do, ladies. Work it.

Dating Success Tips: How To Enchant Him

At this point, he's not interested in our job, family, background, friends, hobbies, or values. He just cares about how we **look**. Don't get angry that men initially think of us as "sex objects", we'll have time for deeper parts of the relationship later, once we've captured them. For now, just play nature's game, and get him **attracted** to you; to WANT you!

Some of us may feel that acting like a woman is something to be ashamed of in a culture of feminism. But unless he's gay, he wants to sleep with a female. So be one. Let your estrogen roll!

Many women protest this approach. You notice this every time we're caught chastising each other:

"Is that all he wants, your body? "

"If he's that shallow, he's not worth it."

"Look at how she dresses!"

"Who does she think she is?"

"He won't respect you!"

"What a pig!"

Modern cultural taboos prevent us from using this genetic trigger and so that we totally miss the fact that if we don't stimulate his eyes properly, we miss a major opportunity to enchant him. But is all this really that distasteful? We've always known that we attract guys with visually sexy appearances. Why do you think we:

- Wear girdles for a more ideal hip to waist ratio

- Wear shoulder pads to mimic good physical conditioning

- Wear tight, revealing, sexy clothing

- And we don't stop there. We'll even commit more extreme physical manipulation to optically attract a male such as:

- Injecting stuff around our eyes, lips and cheeks

- Surgically removing fat and ribs from our body

- Tattooing and putting holes in various body parts

These insights may not be very pleasant to bring up, but our biology doesn't give apologies. Like it or not, this is how we're designed. Fortunately, we don't have to look like a freaking model or the hottest girl on the block to cue a man's visual interest. It just means that a few simple changes could enhance our scoring rate dramatically. Let's look at some tips on how to stimulate a man's **main** sex organ. Chances are you're already using these techniques, but NOW you'll understand the science behind why they work!

Eyes: Paint them.

Why have we been painting our eyes for thousands of years? It takes lot of time. Some of us could get out the door earlier! But perhaps it's not a waste. Science shows that human visual systems differ even from other primates. How? We have more of the white part of our eyes showing! Even more showing than a guy's eyes! This occurs because humans use the eyes for communication more than our other primate cousins do. By lining our eyes and/or adding color to our lids, we enhance our main communication tool. So keep doing this. If you haven't yet, get started.

Lips: Make them red

You already know that lipstick makes your lips appear redder. But why is this important? Here we go with more political-incorrectness, but could it be to stimulate male arousal? For millions of years male mammals were stimulated by the swollen lips of a female's vulva — easily recognized when the female moves around on all fours. The problem is our species learned to stand upright, and that attraction signal became hidden. So scientists think women unconsciously make their facial lips red in color in order to simulate the same effect for human males. Think about it. Why else would we unconsciously want to paint our lips? It makes no sense. And why would a man unconsciously get aroused by that? If you doubt this, just ask any primate researcher about our closest genetic relative, the chimpanzee. The female chimp does in fact attract males by advertising her pink genital swelling when she wants to mate.

Clothing: Stress the female shape.

Use your clothing to accentuate the female shape in those areas that men are programmed to respond to. Stress the good parts and hide the not so good parts. Remember his brain is designed for female shape detection. Work this to your advantage!

High heels: Use 'em.

Though they're hell on your feet, they do promote a lordosis stance. This unconsciously drives him crazy.

Breasts: Expose them.

Legally, that is. Expose skin, show cleavage, protrude nipples or just push them up. It all works. Even if you don't think you have breasts, use the augmented bras now available. They'll promote the same response.

We don't know why breasts so effectively capture a guy's attention, but some scientists theorize that a fixation to a biochemical called Oxytocin is responsible. Others think the human female breast is a unique physical trigger because it is actually a replacement for the buttocks signal, another sexual signal lost when we started walking. According to ethnologist Desmond Morris, standing upright eliminated the sexual signal of the rump that primates normally use, so larger breasts evolved to simulate puffy buttocks in order to attract males. This latter idea could have some merit because women now use silicon to make their breasts look larger (or saline or whatever they're implanting in them these days).

But does playing up breasts work? Researchers say "yes." Having breasts has been so effective for our species that today human females have evolved breasts that are:

- Larger than any other species
- Visible even when the female is NOT lactating to feed a baby!

Exercise and Diet: **You know this.**

If you're already doing it, keep it up. If not, what are you waiting for?

I know that all these techniques to enchant a guy sound manipulative. That's because, well, they are. This explains why many female animals display their physical body to attract males, and why human females have never been immune from this influence. Our female ancestors have been altering body parts to attract males for thousands of years. Even in the 19th century, women used belladonna in their eyes so they would dilate to indicate sexual interest.[38] So, matter how "sophisticated" we think we are, our biology is driving us to look sexy anyway.

Curiously, this instinct accelerates when we are ovulating. Our body actually increases its levels of Estradial at mid-cycle when we are most fertile. What is Estradial? A female hormone that causes us to feel sexy and has been found to correlate with how we dress. This is why when we are at peak fertility we wear more jewelry, make-up, tighter clothing and less of it. Subconsciously, our bodies know we are ready to mate and that influences us to dress for optimal male visual stimulation.[39]

Isn't evolution wonderful?

CHAPTER 5: Dating Phase III - Captivation

Julie and Sally ran into each other the following week at the gym. Sally was wearing some new warm up clothes.

"Hey. I went to that office party."

"But you hate dressing up and wearing make-up and were thinking of not going. Did you wear something sexy?"

"Yeah, but I felt kind of like I was faking it."

"What made you do it?"

"I wanted to test what you told me. It was worth a try.

"And..."

"Well, afterwards a few of us went to a couple pubs and wow! The looks I got! Not only was I noticed, but it definitely felt like I was wanted! Way more guys than normal came over to talk."

"So it's working."

"Yeah, but, Julie, I didn't know what to do other than my normal social routine. What's that last Phase? *Captivation*?"

"That's it. The last step. Getting him to ask you out."

"But aren't women supposed to wait for men to ask?"

"Evolution gave us ways to draw him in. If our female ancestors waited, we'd be extinct!" Julie laughed.

"So what do I do instead?"

"Pull him in. Show him you are interested. Guys are a little dense. They don't get subtle messages very well."

"I've noticed."

"And some might even be gun-shy. So you've got to be clear and direct when you communicate."

"So how does this part work?"

"This time there are 5 steps," Julie said.

Sally pulled a piece of paper and pen from her pocketbook.

Dr. Pat's "Truth": How To Get Him to Ask You Out

Now that he's detected you and he wants you, this final Phase is critical if you want a date. The problem is it's not as simple as him just walking over. Some guys are petrified. Or unsure of whether they're reading you right. Now's when you fix the confusion, but don't ruin it . . .

The Best Way to RUIN Getting a Date

Hidden messages don't work for guys. Captivation requires clear, direct communication. This is YOUR power. Contrary to other advice you may have received, women always had power to attract and capture a man. No need to wait. It's called flirting; a lost art for some.

But today's woman feels afraid to "present" herself by flirting. Some say cultural inappropriateness is to blame, but our research finds a simpler answer - women being afraid to say "no" to casual sex. Therapeutically we say that she would rather be "conquered" (a version of psychological rape in order to avoid responsibility for the sex). But our lack of skill at being self-centered enough to say "no" enables us to "capitulate" and then later blame him for our failure to negotiate equitably and make it safe to approach us.

Would you rather capitulate and be conquered, or be confident enough to negotiate a safe approach for him? If we fear "flirting" in order to let him know he can come closer, we lose the opportunity to create a dating relationship. Shocking as it sounds, this advice works. I see hundreds of women every month effectively kick in this mammalian program and successfully captivate a guy. You will too!

Don's POV: Why Guys Are Morons or Scared.

Talk about "lost in translation!" Dr. Pat identifies here a main factor we guys struggle with every day with women – indirect communication. This distinctly female form of discourse has sabotaged more than one relationship. We guys hear it like:

"How come you didn't notice I wanted to leave the party? Didn't I comment on the draperies?"

"Of course I wanted you to get the groceries. Didn't I say the milk was expired?"

"What do you mean you didn't know I wanted you to mow the lawn? Didn't I ask you if you were playing golf today?"

So even though some books say you shouldn't chase us, the authors clearly can't support their research with any primate studies about how female primates "chase" guys.

Females are designed to show guys that they are available AND interested. The problem with some expert opinions in male/female communication and relationships is they've done no science to back up their opinions. But our hesitancy to approach you should be no surprise. Just look at the world we live in:[42]

If a guy mentions how nice you look, it's sexual harassment...but if he keeps quiet, it's male indifference.

If he appreciates the female form and frilly underwear, he's a pervert ...if he doesn't he's gay.

If he buys you flowers, he's after something...if he doesn't he's not thoughtful.

If he's proud of his achievements, he's full of himself...if he isn't he's not ambitious.

If he tries to keep himself in shape, he's vain...if he doesn't he's a slob.

If he puts a woman on a pedestal and tries to protect her from the rat race, he's a male chauvinist...if he stays at home and does the housework, he's a pansy.

If you have a boring repetitive job with low pay, it's called exploitation...if he has a boring repetitive job with low pay, he should get off his ass and find something better.

If he lets himself be vulnerable, he's a wimp...if he doesn't he's an insensitive bastard.

If he pursues you too much you feel like he's stalking...if he doesn't he's indifferent.

You can imagine why we feel like idiots! We suffer as our 20 million-year-old bodies short-circuit trying to figure out how to fit in to this bizarre new world. Most guys feel awkward, anxious and downright frightened when they have to approach you. Remember that ex-Navy Seal, award-winning body-builder who dwindled into a shriveling mess when he had to approach a girl.

So, take it from a guy. Don't ignore the facts. We need help.

Flirt!

Dating Success Tips: How to Turn Flirting Into Success

And flirt you shall. The following are the major 5 flirting steps, designed by NATURE, not pop-theory, to help you capture the guy you just enchanted.

Step 1: Show Interest

Embedded in your DNA over the past 20 million years is a process designed to lead a male into your territory. Essentially, he solicits attention and you respond to it. It's just that simple. Your body knows how to do this naturally and scientists have found that a guy will solicit or initiate getting your attention by:

- Standing taller
- Pushing his chest out

- Exaggerating his movements. For example, research shows he will stir his drink with his whole arm not just his wrist like he usually does. Or he'll use his whole body to light up a cigarette with elaborate shaking of his arm from the elbow to extinguish a match. He may even swagger like gorillas and other primates do.
- Patting his hair, adjusting his clothes, tugging his chin, in addition to other grooming techniques, to diffuse nervous energy.[40]

When he does that, he's sending the message of "I am here. I am available." This is where YOU come in. Instead of waiting, you must respond (verbally or physically) in a genetically predictable way. This means you've got to do some extra work here. All body visuals speak more to his brain's limbic right lobe (his feminine side) than his neocortical left lobe (masculine, mano-a-mano, talking, teaching, arguing side). Problems occur when we fear appearing vulnerable and use the neo-cortical, talking-mode to control, compete and conquer him. These women then get mad or sad when he either:

• Goes away

• Respects her, but fails to cherish her.

Remember, tearing the wings off butterflies to see how they fly results in no butterfly or flying. Women who know how sensitive men are do not drive them away by negating male energy. He only feels cherished and safe when he is respected. If you want him into you, make him feel that way.

Use common mammalian mating behavior to let him know you are interested. Whether in an Amazonian jungle, a salon in Paris, the highlands of New Guinea, the African bush, an airport in Japan or a pub in Manhattan, these female responses have been recorded by many notable scientists such as Goodall, Givens, Van Hoof and even Darwin. For example, the German ethologist Irenäus Eibl-Eibesfeldt of the Max Planck Institute for Behavioral Physiology[41] secretly photographed female responses to male solicitations around the world and found that men can't resist certain responses. Using these techniques consciously once you've attracted a man's attention demonstrates your interest:

#1 — Smile:

Research found that females smiled and lifted their eyebrows in a swift motion as they opened their eyes in a wide gaze, followed by dropping their eyelids, tilting their head to one side and looking away. So, at least smile at the guy who vies for your attention.

#2 — Act Shy:

Cover your face with your hands and/or giggle nervously or exhibit a coy look by cocking your head and looking up shyly at him. Why does this work? I don't know. Probably because it tells men you're not going to dominate and whip them into submission. You can do that later, after you're married. (Only kidding.)

#3 — Raise your shoulders and/or arch your back:

Here's that lordosis thing again! Lordosis is a fancy way of saying, "stick your butt out." This is the classic "hot babe" pose. Think Marilyn Monroe. Use this technique only for brief moments because you'd look like a prostitute walking around this way all the time. (Which is why they're doing it!)

#4 — Sweep your hair as you look at him:

Tossing your head to fling your hair back in a sweeping motion can also be accompanied by your hand assisting the sweep.

#5 — Make room for him:

If you're surrounded or obstructed by others, move to a clearer area.

#6 — Maintain eye contact for five seconds

It will seem like hours, but it's only five seconds (1001, 1002,

1003...1004......1005...), and that eye-to-eye connection is the best method to let him know you are interested. Of course, if you're not interested in a guy's solicitation — look away. This will indicate that he should step away. So, if interested, show it clearly!

Step 2: Let It Be Safe To Approach

Giving him notice that you're interested doesn't mean you have to pursue him. **Just let him know you are pursuable!** That it's safe for him to approach you. Typically a confident male won't need any further encouragement. But aren't all men this confident? Unfortunately, most men don't just lack assurance, they're terrified. Researchers believe that our modern society has removed rites of manhood from our culture and whip-lashed guys with gender identity and women's liberation issues. The resulting confusion and chaos has made a lot of guys hypersensitive, confused or just plain too scared to put a move on you even if they are interested in you!

You see, **your "selection power" is one of the most dominant in nature's forces over a male.** Our cells know it. So once you've got his attention and shown him you're interested, make it safe for him to approach easily. How close you allow him to get depends on your culture. For Americans:

• Intimate space is about 18 inches around the head for intimate companions and pets

• Personal space is about two to four feet for friends

• Social space about is four to eight feet away for work and social gatherings

• Public space about is nine to ten feet beyond, especially if you have gas.[43]

Allow him to start in your social space and then to slowly move into your personal space. You can pick up our pheromones from a few feet away and this helps you unconsciously determine if you're really attracted to him. The latest scientific research on sweaty T-shirts has found that pheromones like your dad's, but not too much, stimulate arousal. Apparently, if too much like dad's an incest avoidance instinct is triggered.

How to make it safe also depends on the situation, so you're going to have to figure this out for yourself, but here are some ideas:

- Is it easy to get to you? Get off the mechanical bull at the bar or out of the tampon section if you're in the grocery store.

- Lose any guy you're with. (This one should be obvious.)

- Lose your girlfriends. Why? Sometimes he may feel outnumbered if you're with a crowd. More confident guys will notice the leader of the group and approach her to gain insertion into the group. Less confident guys may need you step aside for a moment.

- Face him. You may just need to swing around in your seat.

- Make room. Slide over.

Step 3: Engage Communication

Now that you've drawn him in, you've got to convince him to stay. Otherwise, you'll never capture him for a date. So, in addition to body language, you will need to add verbal communication. But guys suck at this so you'll have to help him talk. His body knows you have all the power in mate selection and is afraid that if he starts to talk he'll blow it and you'll think he's a jerk. He may be a jerk, but you'll figure that out later. Help him get started talking first by making eye contact and smiling. The idea is to get him to approach you and say something — anything. Once he's taken the first hurdle and initiated a conversation, no matter now inane his first comment, you can gently guide the conversation:

#1 — Idle Talk:

It's OK to engage in idle, meaningless conversation. Comment on the weather, the environment, the news, the architecture of the room, the price of the eggs if at the grocery store, selection of beers if at the pub, or anything that comes to mind. Once you're in a longer-term relationship, you'll expect him to stop meaningless conversation for some reason. (He probably won't, but don't bring that up now.)

#2 — Grooming Talk:

Perform what anthropologists call "grooming talk." Ask him if he likes the food. Tell him how you like his job, car, attitude or anything that will make him think you respect him. He needs to know you think he's worth something.

#3 — Synchronize Body Movement:

This will happen naturally so you don't have to worry about it. When you are both comfortable enough, you'll align your bodies face-to-face and begin synchronized body movement and breathing. This synchronization, which also happens when dancing, is classic mammalian behavior in relationships and can even be seen after birth with mothers and babies. Once synchronization occurs, you will have successfully escalated the attraction process and are now faced with an opportunity to enter the capture phase of dating.

Step 4: Plan What's Next (but let him **think** he's **doing it**)

This phase is simple. He's supposed to show you he's interested and ask you to plan future meetings with him like, "I've enjoyed meeting you and am interested in seeing you again. When can we get together?" But it might sound something more like, "Um, I thought, well, listen, maybe we, uh, what if, mmmmm, er, like would you, uh, I mean, [deep sigh, look of panic]." If the latter happens, just say, "Yes!" Act like you heard him. Tell him you'd love to get together and thank him for asking. You'll see a good example of this at the end of the movie *The Incredibles* when the teenage girl hero finally gets approached by the most popular guy in school. He fumbles, she recovers. Touchdown!

These future meetings could be lunch, dinner, a show, a movie, a social event or just coffee. But oddly enough, some guys are afraid to show their interest, which frustrates women to no end. One woman analyzed bad-dating experiences in England and found that guys never expressed interest. She cynically concluded this was due to several reasons: At boarding school the lost affection from their mothers at an early age left them incapable of intimacy with women because:

- They drank too much, which left them incapable of intimacy
- They were repressed homosexuals
- They simply didn't like women

So enable him to express interest. Plant the seeds. Women who don't practice the art of feminine, respectful conversation never plant seeds for future meetings. They require HIM to be courageous. But punks and nerds are courageous, while real men want to be "gentlemen." How do you plant seeds? Try leading questions like:

- "You mentioned that the art museum is bringing in the new exhibit. Do you know the date?"

- "My brother promised to take me to the new play downtown, but had to cancel. I hope my girlfriend will go with me."

When these seeds drop in fertile soil, they blossom. Gentlemen like to help ladies in any kind in distress. If the scientists are right, at this point you've successfully attracted him into you and captured him into a future dating relationship. This may not work 100 percent of the time, but your hit rate will dramatically increase over the option of, well, just waiting.

**There will never be a woman as sensitive inside (anima)
as a man,
nor will there ever be a man as strong inside (animus)
as a woman.**

**A woman who knows how to be a lady is a woman
who presents a receptive, available and respecting
persona to a man rather than a masculine passive-
aggressive ego-driven animus.**

Step 5: Prepare for Sex or **Not**

During future meetings, you'll become more comfortable together and your bodies will know what do from there. But remember, at this point he's only interested in sex! Not love. (Don't forget the earlier chapters?) He generally wants to move fast and doesn't realize you may have different views on how well you need to know someone before you have sex with them (which contrary to a guy is usually longer than dinner). Nevertheless:

— RULE OF DATING —

Women prefer familiarity and commitment before
they have sex with a guy.
Guys have different standards — absolutely no sex
until she says, "Yes."

Now some experts say that guys want to take it slow for a long-term relationship, but chances are you won't be with one. That's because scientific data shows that guys hold off, but only if they have to! If you're ready, few guys will resist. His primal agenda ruthlessly demands that he sow his seed far and wide in order to replicate, and this clashes with your tendency for caution and selectivity. This requires you to make a decision and it's an important decision!

Fast sex rarely becomes solid lovemaking. In therapy, I see this happen. A "claw woman" short-circuits her anxiety at being deflowered by a stealthy man by having a let's-get-it-over-with attitude. This results in either: (1) an addiction to sex fraught with violence of mind, body and spirit, or (2) no friendships past the infatuation superficiality. In this case, sex becomes an animal event – a quickie – versus making love – a human event.

The movie *Quest for Fire* shows the issue of fast vs. slow sex clearly. Having sex (more yang than yin) and/or making love (more yin than yang) are both fine as long as BOTH people want the same style at the same time. **Negotiated sexuality is the secret of mating and/or marriage.** Otherwise, games are being played through intimidation with fear (rape) or seduction with guilt (shotgun wedding). Negotiating manipulates to achieve useful balance, while intimidation and seduction are gamey ways to use or abuse the other person for money, security or sex gratification.

Sex or not, now that you're dating, hold on for a biochemical roller-coaster ride. Even without sex, a hormone rush will make you insane for about ninety days when you'll experience:

- **Time Waste**: We can spend 85-100% doting on each other.

- **Ignorance**: Weaknesses in you will be ignored and you'll appear unique and charming. Later these features will become irritants to him.

- **Fear:** Interestingly, this biochemical rush can be accompanied by paralyzing fear, which may impair normal function.[44] A 19th century French novelist said, "Whenever I gave my arm to Leonore, I always felt I was about to fall and I had to think about how to walk."

Given this state of mind don't — I said don't! — make any rash long-term decisions like asking him to put you on the deed, buy you a car, have you move in, co-sign a loan, etc., until after this hormonal rush is over. Because if you do, he just might do it.

--- SECTION III: Your Dating Toolkits ---

"I did it!" Sally said.

"That was fast. You're dating someone?"

"Not just one. Three!"

Julie laughs. "You seem to be happier than you were a few weeks ago."

"You know, I am. It was awkward at first, but now I feel confident. I don't have to wait and hope."

"Well now you've got a bigger problem," Julie said.

"What problem. I just solved my dating issues."

"Yes, you did. And a good job. But time for caution. Getting a date is just the first step to finding a meaningful relationship. But it doesn't mean you won't get hurt. Now you need to be aware of the dangers."

"I've been hurt before. But maybe it's better than loneliness."

"True, but maybe the pain can be mitigated."

"How do I do that?" Sally asked.

DATING TOOLKIT #1: What To Do Before You Date Him – "Fling" Avoidance Techniques

Now that you've enchanted him, rush into his heart and be carried into the realm of romance and joy forever!

[Cue: Sound of screeching wheels...]

Not so fast. Is he the right one to enchant? Or maybe you didn't enchant him...he seduced YOU in to the relationship! You see, guys may not be smart enough to seduce you consciously, but their bodies are. And our bodies have had millions of years to perfect the game. A guy's body instinctively knows how to trigger you and, if you're not aware of it, you can fall for Mr. Wrong. The seduction game helps spread genetic material, but it also causes pain — *"I don't know what happened. I thought we really had something. I fell in love with him so fast, we had sex, and then he never called again. I was dumped."*

We instinctively react to evolution's unconscious mammalian triggers for seduction. Sound crude? Nature is. But regardless of nature's lack of class, our species survives quite well with these mating strategies ingrained in our DNA. It's time to start making better choices in who you fall in love with by being aware of his main seduction patterns. Fortunately, recent scientific research exposes nature's tricks so you now have a better chance to override your instinctive reactions and avoid a dating mistake. A seduction trick his body uses involves triggering what YOUR body wants in a mate.

The 3 Secrets He Knows Your Body Wants

Laura knew that he wasn't a good fit for her. But, for some reason, she couldn't help it. She'd jump whenever he called her for a date, even though half the time he stood her up — with a good excuse, of course. And when they went out he treated her poorly in front of her friends. Embarrassed, she'd often go home humiliated. She suspected he was even seeing someone else. Why couldn't she leave him?

Laura was seduced by one of the five main biological triggers for falling in love. Being unaware of this, she was relegated to a frustrating and hopeless relationship.

Sound familiar?

We've all had our girlfriends warn you about a guy, yet still fell in love with the wrong man. When it doesn't last, we feel great pain and sadness from the loss. But when another suitor appears, we fall back into the same situation. Even though we have the power nature gave us to select a mate, we still get seduced into falling for the wrong ones. How do they do that to us?

Researchers now understand how guys seduce us. A guy instinctively knows, consciously or unconsciously, that we will fall in love if he triggers what evolution designed us to want more than anything else in him. And what do we women want? Sigmund Freud said, "Everything!" Very funny, but studies like David Buss's Harvard research of 10,000 people in 37 cultures found something quite unique from an evolutionary perspective.[45] Surprisingly different from what the "sensitive" male movement has duped us into believing; we do NOT want nice, kind, touchy-feely, vulnerable, and thoughtful men. (*That sounds more like the description of a woman, doesn't it?*) We want something else:

Success!

Not your success. His! Genetic programming urges human females to want to mate with "successful" guys! Think about it. Ever notice how we're not attracted to losers? Unless we're a chronic "fixer," guys who are failures don't arouse us. Losers don't turn us on. So, seducing us means he must be successful...or at least appear to be. This is bred deeply into his instinctive behavior, and ours.

So even though a guy seeks sexiness in us, we want successful in him; a physical desirability along with his ability to pay for the kids. This makes sense evolutionarily. Mating with guys who had resources to feed and protect the mother and kids was critical. Evolution favored this instinct because women who mated with less supportive guys failed to get such critical resources, and eventually went extinct. The survivors who did get these resources and protection replicated more successfully, and eventually produced the modern woman — us! That's why today a guy's success still turns us on even we don't need it.

— RULE OF DATING —

Guys see women as <u>sex</u> objects.

But women see guys as <u>success</u> objects.

So, when you see a beautiful woman with an unattractive guy, what does that say about him? He's got resources. And why do you think a guy wants to appear smarter than his mate does, whether he really is or not? He wants to be seen as a winner. In a recent study[46] guys and gals were asked what intelligence level they would accept in a "date." The answer: average. But when asked how smart would they have to be for you to have sex the answers changed. Women said: above average. Guys? Below average. Enough said on this point. His strategy to seek success and avoid failure is hardwired into his DNA...and yours!

A Lingering Desire

Isn't a man's success an unnecessary tool in modern societies because many of us are able to survive quite well on our own? And for those us who can't, there's government support? Yes, but remember, our bodies have not mutated to accommodate our modern society, and probably won't for millions of years. In the meantime, the desire for successful guys drives the genetic agenda in us even if we have own resources. Why? It makes sense from nature's perspective. Remember, our female ancestors bore the tremendous burden of:

- A nine-month pregnancy
- A painful birthing process
- Many months of breast-feeding
- Many months of carrying a child until it could walk
- Years of caring until the child was self-sufficient

Those guys successful enough to provide resources got selected more often than losers. Still true today. Most times the gentle, literate, and sensitive artistic carpenter will lose out to the insensitive, rich banker any day. Of course, this is old news:

> *"Girls praise a poem, but go for expensive presents.*
> *Any illiterate oaf can catch their eye provided he's rich.*
> *Today is truly the Golden Age: gold buys honor, gold procures love."*
> —Ovid (2,000 years ago)

Nothing has changed. Some may have a hard time accepting that guys work hard to have a big house, boat, or just more money because they want sex. If females only had sex with total losers, though, how many guys would still make the extra effort? Instead, you'd find more guys living on sidewalks in cardboard condos, pandering for handouts so women would find them attractive. Sure, some guys wouldn't do that, but they wouldn't hold out for more than a month without sex; after seeing their friends getting it more often they'd soon find a place on the sidewalk!

Regardless of the culture or social level, studies find that most guys, about two-thirds, like it when they're admired for their success by a female. This explains some of the patterns we see in modern society like:

- Women have affairs with married men — bachelors are more likely to be losers.
- Human rape is conducted more by unattractive losers than anyone else,[47] the desperate act of a male who has failed to achieve a success profile.
- Success-craving and the hormones that drive it increases significantly during a female's peak fertility cycle, just before or after ovulation![48]

Ironically, we complain that all men want is control, domination and success.
But the reason for this?
Because we require it!

So, in your case, how does he entice you specifically? Your body craves certain success characteristics in a male. Knowing them helps you consciously choose who to date without falling madly in love too quickly, or staying in a relationship too long. Sometimes we make mistakes that are right for our biology, but wrong for our career, family and general well-being. Knowing what to look for helps you avoid them. Three "success" factors really make you fall for a guy: Economics, Genetics, Emotions.

You Want Him Successful Economically

Many of us don't need a financially successful guy because we're successful ourselves or because we feel it's politically incorrect to say so. But biology cannot be ignored. Women who deny this instinct either don't have a relationship or, if they do, one of the partners is miserable.

— RULE OF DATING —

Financial success influences your selection of
him twice as much as it influences his
selection of you.
(No matter what age.)

In studies of thousands of people in multiple cultures, researchers found that there are really only two games people play with each other in relationships. One person mates for money and status, and the other person mates for a sensuous home and a sexually available body.[49] Initially, I was shocked at this assertion, but abundant evidence shows this ancient biological program isn't only limited to humans, but exists in studies of a variety of species.[50] For example, female migratory birds choose males with the best territories. If the old guy gets kicked out by a younger male, the female stays with the new one!

— RULE OF DATING —

Relationship economics is simply the exchange
of money for sex.
Evolution does not apologize for this. The
intention is survival of the gene.
Even though we may disagree with the method,
survive it has indeed!

Many women get angry with me in my seminars when we reference this research. They say it devalues them, or is sexist, or puts us back in the 50's! I agree it sounds crass and makes us angry, but I can't avoid the data. The research evidence is accurate, most of it from female researchers! We can ignore the findings, but what if we accept that it's true? We don't have to agree with the resulting behavior, but if we accept this data could it explain the chronic problems we've been having better than any other relationship theory?

In my therapy sessions, when a client explores the relevance of this research, they find that our deep, unconscious instincts for exchanging sex for resources explains a lot of the problems they've been having. Why do you think prostitution and mistresses are so prevalent in our species, even though the risks are high and include disease, murder, injury and drug addiction?

So ingrained is the "money for sex" game in our species
that even with risks of career, money, crime and family,
the ancient profession of prostitution has been used by 69%
of American men (Kinsey research) with 15% of guys who
use prostitution as a regular sexual outlet; with a more
than ample supply available: 100,000 to 500,000
prostitutes in the U.S.; 130,000 in Tokyo; 230,000 in
Poland, 80,000 in Addis Ababa, Ethiopia.[51]

This data causes emotional pain or rage. I don't meet many women who enjoy seeing the publications on this. But the "Money for sex" strategy isn't a bad thing from nature's evolutionary perspective. Biologically it enhances, not diminishes, mating success. Professor Baker, in his book *Sperm Wars*, says that prostitution is such an effective replication strategy that "on average, we should each need to go back through our family tree no further than the 1820s (seven generations) before finding an ancestor who was born to a prostitute."

Money, however, is only one measure of a guy's economic success that stimulates us. Others include:

Social Status

We instinctively want to marry up. A guy at a higher social level, no matter which culture was studied, turns women on. From an evolutionary perspective, this also makes sense. Being in higher social strata enhances a female's genetic survival because her genes will combine with more successful and/or attractive males. This DNA design still influences modern females today as seen in the Marla Maples and Donald Trump affair, or Michael Jackson's surrogate mothers. So guys wanting to score better tend to hang out in lower social circles.

Age

In all 37 cultures studied, women prefer guys who are older; older men are usually more experienced and successful economically. This pattern reverses, but only in cultures where younger men are already wealthy.

Professional Status

Seen in the workplace every day when a secretary or White House Aid has sex with the boss. A woman's biology drives her to be stimulated by the "success" agenda and a guy's biology drives him to go for it in his career. He can't help it, which is why we find professionals from preachers to presidents getting caught with their pants down. Sexual Harassment and Management Training consultants who fail to consider this mammalian genetic instinct contribute to continued corporate infractions.

Do Men Have More of a Sex Drive Than Women?
Recent research finds this belief to be wrong. Men and women's sex drives are identical, but we get confused because guys get stimulated daily (visually) while women get stimulated infrequently (how many times can he buy her a house?). For example, I encountered one female with no sexual activity for years who shared that she became sexually aroused when the guy she was dating prepaid her apartment rent for the season.

You Want Him Successful Genetically

Genetic success in his physical body turns us on too. Why? These characteristics show us his potential for providing us resources and economic capacity; not unusual for animals, even if these genetic characteristics prove to be burdens. For example, consider the larger tail on a male peacock. It handicaps the poor bird in hiding or escaping predators. But he has no choice if he wants sex. The drab colored females, safe in their camouflage, choose the guy they want — and do they want a guy with genetics for being a predatory target! Why would a female want to mate with a bird carrying such a survival disadvantage? Researcher Amotz Zahavi[52] in the *Journal of Theoretical Biology* says it's precisely because if the poor sucker is still alive he must have some survival advantage! With such a large handicap, the female figures this guy must have something on the ball because he's still walking around! He must be superior at escaping predators, finding food, resisting disease etc. So the increased mating opportunities for the peacock far outweigh the disadvantage of the tail.

This explains why guys do stupid things to prove superiority over other guys. It so we will select them! As we mentioned earlier in the book, ever notice young guys exposing themselves to risks or dangers like fast driving, potent drugs, drunkenness, extreme sports and other unsafe behaviors? Scientists believe they are unconsciously saying to females, "I must be strong and superior enough if I can do these drugs, or swallow this alcohol and endure a hangover, or risk my life in no fear activities and still remain alive and healthy." Unfortunately, humans have longer lives than most animals so the consequences of this show-off behavior may be detrimental. A drunk youth who drives fast to impress his female finds all too often that being wrapped around a telephone pole hinders mating opportunities.

So, what are the physical, genetic success factors we look for in mate selection?

Size and Strength

Tall men have more mating success in all cultures studied. Size provides more physical protection for the female and an increased capacity for success (economically and physically), so tall guys have an advantage. This also helps profitability in the platform-shoe market.

Health

That's why many guys get to the gym and trash the Twinkies.

Symmetry[53]

Interestingly, left and right side body symmetry is important probably because asymmetry could be due to genetic defects or health issues. So women will unconsciously, but instinctively, look for symmetry in a guy's body. A study of 200 college students found that guys with high symmetry reported more sexual partners than asymmetrical guys. Conversely, a guy's fascination with female breast symmetry may stem from a similar assessment of a woman!

Good Looks

Studies show that other females wanting him validates a guy's genetic "success;" which explains why women want a guy more if other women also want him. This is not limited to humans; most mammalian studies find the same pattern across many species.[54] Good looking males, knowing they have an advantage, can be very promiscuous and tend to leave their females holding the bag with the chores and child-rearing. Why do we still hang around with such men even though our girlfriends tell us we're crazy? We can't help it; it's in our genetic program. Female instincts still promote this choice of mate because even though he will be a selfish, lazy and conceited nerd, her offspring will likely be attractive as well, which gives her genes an advantage in replicating. So, if you're going out with a jerk, make sure he's a good-looking one.

Penis length

Yes, like Woody Allen said, penis envy shouldn't be limited to women. But why penis length? Remember, if a woman mates with a large "package," then her offspring will likely have more success in replicating her genes. This has to do with genetic warfare regarding sperm displacement (topic of a later book).

You Want Him Successful **Emotionally**

His emotions are also important to us if they are Success-oriented. Research indicates the following items are key triggers:

Ambition/Industriousness:

Yes, we want to see if he's willing to do hard work. Sheer hard work is the best predictor of success: higher salaries, better education, promotions, etc.

Dependability/Stability:

We want him to be dependable. Why? Unreliable guys threaten our resources because they are more self-centered, possessive, dependent, jealous, abusive (verbally and physically), inconsiderate and moody. They also tend to monopolize shared resources and have more affairs.

Intelligence

If he's smart he could be more successful, but we cannot be too discriminating here. If he's a bit smarter than us that could be a problem
because guys generally seek similarities in intelligence when it comes to long- term mates, unless, of course, they're on the "trophy wife" plan.

Compatibility

Values need to be aligned to promote long-term relationship success and access to successful resources.

Love and Commitment

We want fidelity so that males focus their successful resources on our children and us.

Success Trumps Sensitivity

The common belief that women prefer sensitive, emotional males is wrong. Scientists say the studies supporting this myth failed to consider the female's genetic driver — success.
Instead of asking about preferences for a sensitive versus an insensitive male, they should ask if the female would mate if he had a great house, or if she would have access to a large annual sum of money,
or if their kids would be totally protected financially, or if she would be the envy of women for landing such a successful guy.
In these cases, the answers are different. Success turns on women, and this explains why unattractive men can really land some attractive females, and why some females marry the least sensitive guys.

These success triggers don't diminish once you've fallen in love with him. He needs to keep it up even after marriage. One study found no link between money and sex after marriage (the study did not study sex with mistresses), but other studies quickly contradict this finding. For example, sexual dysfunction occurs more in men with declining income levels. If a guy's income drops more than 20%, she will have 60% more problems becoming aroused by him when compared to a guy whose income went up![55]

It's important for keeping him in a relationship that you remember how these factors affect him as well. When we women feel financially independent, we might tend to not appreciate financial success in him and just go for sex. That's fine, but wanting sex and money is narcissistic. We would do better to respect men even when we have our own money; live at his level, not ours, unless we want to be the man-energy in the relationship. For example, in the book *The War Against Boys*,[56] Christina Sommers shares stories about the damage young masculine women do when they make young men (sons, students, grandsons) feel ashamed of their competitive, conquering and controlling nature. Morality that is scheduled toward women's nature — i.e., comfort over conquest — undermines men who need to have conquest over comfort.

Women need to feel good to do good; men need to do good to feel good.

Today, a lot of us women think they want a "feeling" man, but the price for such a "man" is that the we must now be the competitor, conqueror and controller in the relationship. Men who like to be respected avoid women who act like men. Men (boys, really) who like their women strong avoid women who like to be cherished. This is nature's dance and it plays out in all our seductions. Being aware helps us avoid selection and relationship mistakes. But how can we detect his "success" strategies for seducing us?

Remove His Mask: How To Tell If He Wants Casual Sex or a Permanent Partner

Scientists find that effective seduction in animal mating occurs through a ritual they call "Display Strategies." Like all the other primate instincts you've seen so far, humans are not immune to this either. If a guy wants to mate with you, he makes you think he's not a loser and that you'll greatly enhance your genetic code surviving into the future by mating with him. So he does what all mammals do when they want to mate — he displays the success that he innately knows you seek!

Display strategies explain why guys overspend on things like flashy cars, stylish clothes, gold chains, sunglasses, cool music and other fashion symbols. Every generation is alarmed by the next generation's dress, dancing, music, walking patterns, language, hair, etc., but it's all just a bunch of young sex- fevered guys trying to get laid by looking "cool" (successful). Unrelenting as we get older, this instinct still influences a guy's choice in cars, houses, clothes

and if he can afford it, accessories like sports equipment, off-road vehicles, weapons, boats, planes, etc. If he appears successful enough, a guy knows you'll overlook his imperfections because your hormones are also rushing and you'll think his quirks are cute — not irritants like you'll discover later once it's too late and you're already in love with him.

For example, a typical guy also uses food as a Success Display. Not a new idea. Even before dinosaurs, males displayed success by providing a resource like food to the female. Courtship feeding is a very effective way to display success because it shows the female how good the male is as a hunter, provider and worthy partner.[57] We see this throughout nature:

- A male scorpion brings a gift, usually food such as a dead insect and, if accepted, mates with the female while she's eating. This of course inspires the male to bring lots of food. If after the necessary 20 minutes of sex there's food left, however, both fight over the scraps remaining.
- The Black-Tipped Hag Fly sets out a juicy meal to attract a female and then mounts her before she's done eating.
- The male roadrunner displays a dead rat, but only gives it to her AFTER she has sex with him.
- Flies bring aphids or spiders.
- Birds bring fish or lizards.

- Chimps bring animal flesh.
- Humans…well, guys bring meat too. Usually steak or lobster.

Even though buying food is one way a guy demonstrates success to stimulate your prehistoric genetic instincts, if you're a "liberated" woman you can mess it up! How? By insisting on picking up the dinner check — thereby sabotaging the mating ritual! If you want equality, keep it in the office. But if you want to cut the relationship short, go ahead and pull out your credit card.

— RULE OF DATING —

"Liberated" females who try to find Mr. Right are
usually lonely because they keep
stepping on biology.

In addition to food, there are many other options a guy uses to display success to you. In his book *The Evolution of Desire: Strategies of Human Mating*, David Buss's extensive scientific research[58] reveals that the following display strategies work best:

Male Display Strategies for Attracting <u>Casual Sex</u> Partners:

- Displaying wealth and the willingness to part with it (giving money away to charities, street people, etc.)
- Flashing money
- Buying gifts (the more expensive the better, but not too much less they take it for granted)
- Taking you out to an expensive restaurant (without the sexual mounting, please)
- Wearing expensive clothes
- Sucking in his stomach
- Buying a mixed drink (something better than beer or wine)
- Giving the waitress a large tip
- Displaying self-confidence
- Calling the shots (taking control, instead of "whatever you like, honey")
- Acting macho

- Be seen as being wanted by other women
- Having a nice car
- Having a car with loud music. Guys make song just like other species: frogs croak, crickets chirp, cats howl, porcupines whine, alligators bellow, elephants rumble, geckos chip, and young human adolescents annoyingly turn up music devices in public places. (If these guys knew that this signals that they're not getting enough sex would they lower the volume?)
- Bragging about his accomplishments while sucking in his stomach
- Showing off
- NOT being sexually overt
- Displaying physical prowess while sucking in his stomach.
- Flexing muscles
- Opening jars
- Playing sports (better if the sports are testosterone-driven such as mountain climbing, football, motorcycles or anything that involves sweat)
- Lifting weights
- Having a deeper voice (apparently this makes you women weak in the knees because it indicates higher levels of male hormones)[59]
- Boasting
- Did I mention sucking in his stomach?

Male Display Strategies for Attracting <u>Permanent</u> Partners:

- Showing potential for having resources
- Studying hard
- Describing ambitions goals
- Wearing expensive clothes
- Still sucking in his stomach
- Showing love, commitment and devotion
- Discussing marriage
- Showing deep concern for your problems and sensitivity to your needs
- Showing emotional support
- Showing that he will be there for you in times of need
- Showing persistence and willingness to sacrifice his time to

pursue you
- Showing that he is helpful (like opening doors, sitting down last, fixing stuff, etc.)
- Showing kindness
- Being protective of you by acts like putting his arm around you in a crowd, holding your hand while crossing a street, asking someone not to blow smoke in your direction
- Appearing vulnerable
- Being polite and considerate of others
- Showing that he likes kids
- Showing loyalty
- Saying "I love you"

But do these things really work on us? Research of 100 newlywed women confirmed that their husbands used these displays 100% of the time during courtship.

Does all this sound manipulative?

It is. But as you've learned by now: Nature doesn't care. Evolution only cares about the result — more babies carrying our genetic material into the future. As we've seen before, this ancient phenomenon exists as a program in your DNA too! You're not going to change it anytime soon. Even if he's a nice guy, losers statistically go home alone more than successful guys.

If you then avoid a "fling", and start dating, you now want to evaluate whether he's worth it in the long-term. That's next.

DATING TOOLKIT #2: How To Tell If He's Worth It – The Guy Profiling Tool

After you begin dating, step back and take a moment to assess how the man of the hour is trying to impress you with his "success" or capacity for it. Noticing his moves gives you a chance to evaluate whether you want to fall for him any further or not. Notice how your body is responding. Then ask yourself, do I want him for him, or am I getting sucked in to a relationship I don't want? The following profile tool can help.

Falling-In-Love Success Assessment Tool

(Put a check mark for each row. Total the number per column at the bottom)

His Characteristics	1 Poor	2	3	4	5 Great
Net worth					
Earning capacity					
Social status					
Age					
Size and strength					
Health					
Symmetry					
Good looks					
Ambitiousness					
Dependability					
Intelligence					
Compatibility					
If sexually active, penis length (be honest)					
Ability to love and commit					
Capacity to touch					
Self-confidence, machismo					
Desired by other women					
Bragging rights; accomplishments					
Kindness, helpfulness					
TOTAL AVERAGE OVERALL COUNT					

Key Questions About Your Profile Results

- Do you want him or the food he brings and the restaurants he takes you to?

- Is he a nice guy or does he just have nice resources (car, boat, house or other material possessions)?

- Are you impressed with his life values or just his talents? Or fame?

- Does he show you off, but not cherish you?

- Do his good looks overshadow the fact that he doesn't have a job?

- Are you so infatuated with his money and looks that you can't hear your girlfriends' complaints?

These questions and the profile tool, along with cutting down on the touching and the chocolates, will help you step back and assess the situation before you fall for him too fast. How does he rate in the success dimensions as compared to other guys competing for you? Or, if you're married, how does he rate against other males in the community you are part of?

DATING TOOLKIT #3: What To Do Before You Sleep With Him: Nature's Drug Test

He attracted you because he appeared successful, but nature gives him other seduction tricks. Ignorance of nature's seductions provides just more material for relationship books. It's time to go deeper. The question really is not WHY men seduce you – we know it's the evolutionary drive to mate – but HOW do does it happen? Knowing the answer helps you remain in control of the "mate selection" process. The answer is simple – he gets you chemically attached to him (no matter how appropriate or inappropriate the relationship may be). Our bodies began manufacturing biochemical drugs millennia ago. Indeed, their impact on our emotions and behaviors laid the foundation for our relationships as long as we've been a species with genders. Let's look at a few.

How He Gets You Infatuated - Dopamine

Our female hormones and brain are designed to mix an exciting drug cocktail to produce a thrilling rush when we meet someone of interest.[60] Scientists can measure these love markers as they stimulate specific brain regions such as — here's a mouthful — the medial insula, anterior cingulated and the basal ganglia.[61] These brain areas contain lots of receptors for our body's biochemical drugs. One particularly interesting one is dopamine, the drug for euphoria, craving...and addiction.[62] This dopamine rush helps us to overlook his flaws, which otherwise might cause us to run away, and helps us focus only on hormonally responding to him.[63]

But what happens after 90 days? By then, this drug begins to wear off, and is supplanted with other endorphins that act more like morphine, serving to calm us down.

— RULE OF DATING —

Everybody falls in love with their soul mate
...for 90 days!

For guys, brain chemistry is designed to:

- Go insane with infatuation in order to fall in love when they first meet you.

- Become attached to you so that they can bond in endless love.

- Reach eventual restlessness and an urge to move on.

Even today's tribes recognize this biological program for love. Anthropological research documents a !Kung woman (the !Kung are a tribe in the Kalahari Desert) folk saying: "When two people are first together, their hearts are on fire and their passion is very great. After a while, the fire cools and that's how it stays."[64] Many ancient cultures like the Romans considered this "falling-in-love" feeling a form of insanity. They were probably right. Research published in the scientific journal Ethnology shows that 87 of 168 societies are aware of this insanity,[65] and you see it in your friends when they fall in love. They go nuts! And so do you. First, you become so enthralled in the new relationship you do crazy things. You might even dump your close friends and not see them again for months!

What other drugs cause seduction? Only parts of an entire system; other drugs guys use to influence you to "fall in love" include one of the main players – Oxytocin.

How He Gets You to Bond – Oxytocin

Ever wonder what makes us want a guy so much and what causes so much pain when we break up? The reason we bond with a guy[65] is due to the neuropeptide Oxytocin, which binds to limbic cells in our brain.[67] Studies on monkeys by Dr. C. Sue Carter[68] of the University of Maryland found this "bonding glue" critical for falling in love. When scientists suppress Oxytocin in a female, she rejects outsider babies. Some scientists think that the existence of Oxytocin, only found in mammals, explains why "love" may have been essential in the evolutionary development of our species.

The power of this love potion shows itself across species from sheep, to monkeys, to humans. Injections of Oxytocin produce a similar range of reactions such as:

- Sheep adopting other infants for mothering
- Human females becoming an "earth mother" and loving the whole world
- Virgins becoming maternal within thirty minutes.[69]

In addition to being the "love" hormone, Oxytocin also exercises a number of other versatile effects on your body:

1. Lust

2. Breastfeeding: Starts the milk let-down response and causes us to automatically leak milk from their breasts when we hear a baby cry — embarrassing in checkout lines.

3. Labor: A natural labor inducer; doctors use Oxytocin injections to speed up contractions in us.

4. Stops Bleeding: Oxytocin reduces postpartum uterine bleeding.

5. Memory Loss: Curiously, Oxytocin makes us forget. Useful for forgetting things like the pain of childbirth — and that last painful breakup with a boyfriend.

6. Logic Breakdowns: Oxytocin stops us from reasoning rationally.

7. Nipple Erections: Dr. Crenshaw refers to a company, Syntocinon, that found Las Vegas show girls were using its Oxytocin nose spray to make their nipples erect.

Because guys don't have much to do with labor or lactation, and bonding, they have less Oxytocin response than we do. Well, except for one moment when guys actually feel an Oxytocin level closer to what we feel:

Ejaculation

Yes, a guy needs Oxytocin to climax. After he ejaculates, however, his Oxytocin level drops rapidly and the overdose he just got makes him feel stoned and lethargic. Then, testosterone's effect once again emerges, making him want to be alone. This is why a guy always feels like rolling over and going to sleep after sex. We don't feel this way because we're used to higher Oxytocin levels.

How a Guy Raises Our Oxytocin Level

A guy triggers our Oxytocin by doing the one thing we love him to do:

Touching Us.

No, not there! I mean like our hand, arm or some other socially acceptable body part. Our Oxytocin level also rises when we *think* about him. Why do you think he gives you flowers, pictures or something to take home to remind you of him? But when he physically touches you, Oxytocin soars! Not only limited to romance, bonding through touch occurs with family, friends, babies, etc.

This is common in many species. Most primates use touching for bonding rituals. But you shouldn't try to duplicate all primate behavior. Capuchin monkeys stick fingers up each other's noses for long periods[70] (not recommended for humans on the first date).

We need touch more than men do. Researchers Barbara and Allan Pease[71] found that "Western women are four to six times more likely to touch another woman in a social conversation than a man is likely to touch another man." When we women get angry we say, "Don't touch me!" Now you know why.

— RULE OF DATING —

Under stress guys avoid touch, but women need it —
not for sex, but for intimacy.

Touch doesn't mean much to him, but it's very important to us because even though the human skin has 2.8 million receptors for pain, 200,000 for cold and 500,000 for touch, our skin is ten times more sensitive than his! There are two very good reasons:

- He evolved running through jungles, hunting and warring...but we evolved cuddling and hugging children

- Estrogen facilitates Oxytocin reactions. His minimal estrogen level diminishes the effect for him...until he ejaculates.

Because of its powerful and contradictory effects on us, I call Oxytocin "God's second joke (Estrogen is His first)." Deciding how to evaluate the impact of Oxytocin as good or bad depends on your situation, your state of mind, and most importantly, who you're with at the moment. Sometimes we want to bond, and sometimes we don't. A low Oxytocin level makes us less likely to bond with a guy, and that's OK as long as his level is low too. But if his Oxytocin is high enough, you could wind up with a stalker. Vice-versa and you'll just become another chapter in a "he's just not that into you" story.

How He Gets You To Fall In Love – PEA

PEA (phenyl ethylamine), a natural amphetamine which occurs at the end of nerve cells, emerges as another biochemical culprit for seducing us by helping impulses jump between neurons in our brains and creating that lovin' feeling. Ever found yourself behaving like a hopeless romantic? Singing in the shower? Walking on air with your heart racing, palms sweating, pupils dilating and a funny feeling in your stomach? That's PEA at work. If a guy can increase our level of PEA, he's ready to seduce us! A high PEA level does interesting things to our body:

- Pulls us into infatuation like we're on a speed drug feeling elation, exhilaration and euphoria.

- Makes us do stupid things like stay up all night to watch the sunrise in the morning with him before we have breakfast and finally go to sleep.

- Diminishes our appetite. That's why we eat less when we fall in love — better than Atkins! That's also why PEA is used in diet pills.

- Makes us absentminded, giddy, optimistic and gregarious.

But PEA can also make us lovesick. A couple psychiatrists, Dr. Michael Liebowitz of the New York State Psychiatric Institute and his colleague Dr. Donald Klein, think that love-sickness in people may be due to PEA depletion causing craving for more of it, just as if someone was addicted to crack or heroin. People with this addiction seek any kind of love affair and, when it ends badly, fall into depression and broken heartedness. Then, in desperation, they seek a new fix in another bad relationship. By stimulating PEA production in such people, scientists have found that these addicts actually stabilize. After years of unsuccessful therapy to "get in touch" with himself, PEA treatments finally prompted one guy to start choosing partners more carefully and avoid the chronic love affair disasters to which he had previously subjected himself.[72]

PEA is great for feeling in love. Unfortunately, there's a down-side. After two to three years in a relationship, love wanes because our brains can't maintain the revved up state from PEA rushes for an extended period of time. Relationship experts tell you he's "just not interested" or "he fell out of love," but they fail to explain why. Well, now you know. The feeling of falling in love is the result of a natural biological mechanism...and an effective design for genetic replication.

PEA can't be stimulated as easily as touching. We have to ingest it. Lucky for guys, they can get us to ingest it quite easily. PEA is readily available in the local food store in diet soft drinks and chocolates! That's why evolution designed guys to bring chocolates on a date! You think men are being romantic, but they're just trying to adjust our biochemical levels.

Can you increase PEA levels in a guy? Sure, just like OXYTOCIN, it spikes naturally in his bloodstream during, of course, orgasm.

— RULE OF DATING —

Falling in love never lasts. Eventually nerve
endings become habituated and PEA levels drop.

Evolution designed you to mate briefly, not
long-term,

and is why longer-term relationships require
much more work.

DATING TOOLKIT #4: What To Expect When Sex Is Imminent – Darwin's Mating Dance Map

No matter what the romantics and poets say, falling in love results from a hormonal potion evolution designed to drive you to — you guessed it — increase your genetic replication rate. This biochemical formula produces a brilliant mating dance. The best way to use this is to be aware of it so you don't follow it blindly. Knowing what to expect provides you with more control and better mate-selection choices. The steps to the dance are:

1. You show up on his radar.
2. He gets enchanted by you and his testosterone drives him to
3. lust for you.
4. You capture him into a dating relationship because you read this book!
5. On a later date, you are alone and as you get physically closer, your pheromones are detected, which actuate other biological processes in his body and hopefully yours.
6. At some point, sex may become imminent. If so, read the rest.
7. Nitric oxide is produced to give him an erection.
8. Oxytocin releases and PEA spikes causing him an orgasm and he suddenly finds himself inside an intense loving experience.
9. He wants to bond with you endlessly as he realizes you are his soul mate and he finally wants you forever by his side in the most passionate and committed relationship.
10. Vasopressin kicks in making him focus intensely on only you and he "falls in love."
11. Feeling fades away in about seven seconds.
12. Nitric Oxide subsides in his bloodstream and his erection goes soft.
13. Your Oxytocin stays high and causes you to feel an even deeper love and bonding with him as his Oxytocin drops making him feel distant and drowsy while his testosterone causes him to want to be alone again. He rolls over and falls asleep.
14. His Vasopressin also returns to normal. But is he into you?
    a. If his Vasopressin is low, he's thinking about how to leave without getting you angry, and will wonder what your

name was several weeks later.

b.   If his Vasopressin is high he'll be a candidate for monogamy. With high Oxytocin, you'll greatly bond into a perfect couple.

Apologies if this sounded cold and distant. Describing the elements of the human mating dance in such a straightforward, logical and scientific manner makes many women angry. It seems that Evolution's cold, selfish hand rarely engenders warm feelings inside us. Guys, on the other hand, just wonder what all the fuss is about. One time when reviewing this research data with a mixed group, the women started yelling in protest about how this isn't the way it is and it should never be published. But the guys? They all said, "Finally, somebody said it!"

Yet despite the wide chasm that exists between the sexes in our perceptions of what happens as we meet and mate, for some reason women from Venus continue to fall in love with men from Mars. They have relationships that deepen into intimacy, and often into marriage; marriages that sometimes prosper for decades. Only now, at long last, we have an explanation of what is REALLY happening, and why it happens.

DATING TOOLKIT #5: How To Tell If He Loves You? The Love Test Method

Are relationships just a cold sexual replication agenda driven by genetic warfare? What about falling in love? We want to bang our heads against a wall hearing that guys see most of the relationship as sexual. But don't interpret this as devaluing you as a person; such thoughts reinforce eating disorders and encourage women to risk their lives with dangerous surgeries so they can look sexy. Avoiding or denying the obvious, however, hasn't worked either, has it? Sure, men seek other virtues than sex in a woman...when they want kids and need help making sure their genetic material survives and prospers. But not now. You're just dating.

When in "dating mode," virtuous qualities in a
mate are the last thing on a man's mind;
even though they might be the first ones on yours!
Until you accept this, his sexual agenda can be
downright hurtful.

Wouldn't it be wonderful if love and romance also fit in with evolutionary genetics? Wouldn't be great if somehow our warm passions and deep longings could also be found in the cold, shallow findings from our laboratories and sweaty field research teams?

Good news. Even though man's insatiable sexual intensity can be validated, so can romance novels and heartfelt longings. The problem with finding love is that we've been ignoring our biology, as if our culture can override it and make it vanish into history. If this were possible then we wouldn't be so shocked when our phone doesn't ring, or he gawks at another woman, or a respected leader of church or state is caught with his pants down. The point is that it's not possible to ignore biology. But instead of allowing this to unconsciously influence us, we can accept it and use it to our advantage. That's why we wrote this book. Finally, what has been missing in our attempts to find and keep a satisfying relationship with all the warmth and cherishing that brings can now be developed on the genetic foundation we've built so far.

Is Love in Our Genetic Nature, or Just Nurtured by Our Culture?

Are we driven by our biology or nurtured by our culture to fall in love. Well, arguing genetics versus cultural norms will linger for years, but recent research answers the question: love is also genetically designed into our biology. This makes sense. Without love and romance humans would stop sex altogether; and we hardly get along now anyway. Have you checked out the grocery store magazines that expose the latest break-ups?

But in the middle of this war and the dysfunctional relationships that consume our gossip columns, something truly amazing happens. Even though nature designed our bodies for battle...it also designed us to fall in love. Falling in love is part of the great Darwinian game, a game so powerful that our species produces abundant literature on the topic. We spend billions annually on love and romance. Love stories permeate the stage, the movies, television, even art and music, while bestsellers about finding that special "soul-mate" abound.

— RULE OF DATING —

We are designed for cold, selfish sex, but our hearts
are programmed for love.
Perhaps this paradox drives our survival as a
species.

You see, love and romance are not contrary to our biology, they are
designed for it! What do you think inspires us to mate anyway! Sex, love
and emotional attachment share so much of the same hormone and brain
configurations that some scientists think our "love" emotions were
absolutely critical for our evolutionary survival.

— RULE OF DATING —

Love's got a lot to do with it!
Otherwise, we wouldn't mate at the rate we do!
Love ensures successfully genetic replication.

A Definition of Love, Finally

How can we define love? It would be a shame to venture this far
without addressing the loaded question that has filled philosophy books
for over five thousand years. We've looked extensively at how and why
love occurs the way it does for humans — but what exactly is love? Some
say that it's a story we invent and then we seek someone who can fill that
story. Others say it's about compatibility and how love can be
manufactured from that. But wouldn't it be great if we had something
more solid: a definition that is concrete and measurable? With
evolutionary genetics we can finally create that definition by first realizing
that:

— RULE OF DATING —

Love is what females give sex for.

Sex is what guys give love for.

This can make us angry, but suspending our anger just a bit allows a deeper question. Is it so wrong to think that women give sex in order to get and keep love? And that guys give love in order to get and keep sex? Accepting this exchange of love and sex brings us to a powerful definition of love itself. Research in this area uncovered probably the best definition for love ever developed:

— THE DEFINITION OF LOVE —

"The only way you know you love yourself or anyone else is

by the contracts you are willing to make and keep."

That's it. Love is saying "I will do it," and meaning what you say and doing what you mean. The type of agreements we are willing to make with each other, and how well we keep those agreements, is perhaps the clearest measure of love.

So, do you love him?

Have you kept your agreements with him?

Has he with you?

"There is no such thing as an older woman. Any woman of any age, if she loves, if she is good, gives a man a sense of the infinite."

—Jules Michelet (1798–1874)

DATING TOOLKIT #6: How To Protect YOU!!! – The Birth Control Debate Solution

If you choose sex remember that, much more than him, you're really choosing to conceive or not. In other words, you're choosing to commit to a family or not. **He can split, you can't.** This is a critical choice given how effective our species is in creating more little humans.

Playing Russian Roulette with your eggs
and a guy not ready to be a dad and support you is a failure of his
manhood and your common sense.

Be a Pro When It Comes to Procreation

Humans are in heat constantly, not seasonally like other mammals. So when you mate with him, remember your body doesn't know about modern-day cultural taboos; it's still operating seven millions years before Trojans (the condom, not the army). So, make sure to use birth control when you're mating. If you doubt how effective our replication rate is, we refer you to the insights from Dawkins book *The Selfish Gene*.[81] Our capacity to procreate is so well honed that he calculated the replication rate of Latin America's three hundred million people; many undernourished, and found that if this population continued to increase at its present rate:

- In five hundred years, they would carpet the whole continent standing shoulder-to-shoulder,
- In one thousand years, each of these people would have one million other people standing on top of his or her shoulders,

- In two thousand years, this mountain of people would have expanded at the speed of light and reached the edge of the known universe.

This should answer any doubts you have about your ability to become impregnated. And if you need more evidence, remember that studies show Latin American culture supports using birth control![82] Worldwide, people are having kids when they don't want them or when their society cannot support them.

Convincing people to use more birth control would be great, but many in a politically correct society feel that birth control is immoral and unnatural. That we shouldn't use it ourselves, or certainly not provide it to other countries. They prefer more *natural* methods. The only problem is they don't know nature's *natural* methods.

Natural Methods?

If you happen to meet these people advocating natural methods of birth control, please inform them that "natural" methods for managing overpopulation are:

- Starvation
- Plague
- War

Clearly, contraception is unnatural, but highly preferable to the alternatives. The United Nation's latest forecast of the world's population in 2050 has dropped from 9.4 billion to 8.9 billion and is expected to stabilize at 9 billion by 2300. This is due to women having fewer children, but also due to war, starvation and, of course, disease — primarily AIDS. Fortunately this prevents the world's population hitting 134 trillion![83]

Politically, some believe we should still let replication continue and argue "but we are civilized and have created welfare to help these people so they don't have to use birth control." Let's review this logic. Birth control is unnatural, but welfare isn't? Saving the children, but not stopping their parents from having more children is a solution? Unfortunately this philosophy only temporarily delays an uncomfortable and inevitably miserable death for millions.[84]

People who are against birth control never suffered from starvation, plague, or war (and have likely been spared the luxury of welfare dependency). However, the millions that have suffered would vote for birth control, but...they're dead. I'm not saying that people who have more children than they can afford are consciously putting the world at risk; they're probably just ignorant of the consequences. It's the intelligent, educated leaders and institutions allowing the practice who are responsible   for   this   situation.

Ancient Practices

Birth control is not a new modern "unnatural" invention:

- For centuries women have been placing fruit, leaves, even crocodile dung, in their vaginas to prevent pregnancy.

- A whole range of herbal drugs were commonly used for birth control in ancient Greece and Rome.

- Evidence of chemical contraception stretches back as far back as four thousand years ago to writings on Egyptian papyri.

- Juvenal, the Roman satirist, wrote about how "we have sure-fire contraceptives" 2,000 years ago.

- Over 2,000 years ago Pliny suggested rubbing sticky gum over the penis before intercourse for birth control.

- The use of a sheath to cover the penis has been known even before Roman times.

- Gabrielle Fallopius designed the first medicated linen sheath in the 1500s, but the item took its name from the personal physician to King Charles II, the Earl of Condom, who recommended its use as an aid to prevent the contraction of syphilis.

Nature's best birth control method, however, is something we still use today — Stress. Miscarriages and missed fertilizations increase dramatically with female stress, which is sometimes manifested as anorexia — an effective way to stop ovulation and menstruation. (The majority of anorexics — 75 percent — emerge from the condition to live a normal and healthy life.)

Throughout human history, "natural" family planning has been and still is infanticide. In hunter-gatherer tribes, about 7% of children are killed by their mothers. According to the World Health Organization, this was the prevalent form of family planning in late 19th-century Britain. Tragically, we still see this in our species when a mother kills her children because she cannot raise them due to a new boyfriend, poor financial situation, depression (likely from environment or biochemical imbalance), close births, twins, lack of a helpful mate, pair-bond instability, lack of resources, etc. These are horrible episodes that are not acceptable and a sign that we need to understand our genetic nature better so that we can prevent such tragedies in the future.

Surprisingly, humans are not the only mammals practicing birth control. Female chimpanzees, for example, know when to chew certain leaves that contain contraceptive chemicals. Amazingly, without modern contraceptives, our hunter-gatherer ancestors were able to plan families and raised only three to four children in their lifetimes. Some, such as the Andamanese, were able to delay their first child until the woman was about 28 years old.[85]

Modern Challenges

Women's designed effective contraceptive devices to prevent unwanted pregnancies in undesirable situations as a practice of "family planning" for thousands of years. Modern women inherited these traits from their mammalian ancestors. Ironically, however, our "modern" contraceptives don't seem to be doing the job. Just look at their failure rate.

- Every year 3% of women have an abortion in the U.S.; according to the Center for Disease Control and Prevention over one million abortions were performed in the U.S. in 1995.
- Estimates elsewhere are ten million abortions in China, four million

in Russia, 300,000 in Japan and about 150,000 in England and Wales.

- According to the World Health Organization, 50% of all pregnancies worldwide are unplanned and 25% are "certainly unwanted."[86]

More irony...Modern technology eliminated one of the most effective natural contraceptives — lactation. Evolution made it difficult for breast-feeding women to conceive. It is hard enough to carry one child while walking long distances or gathering food, water and firewood. Carrying two kids would make it impossible. So evolution produced our genetic design to delay fertilization during the breastfeeding cycle, which turns out to be about four years. Why that length of time? Because at that time the child can walk on its own. Unfortunately, thanks to modern technology, bottle-feeding eliminates this natural contraception, so women can now become fertile much earlier than four years after a birth.

Our modern lifestyle eliminates yet another natural contraceptive — youth. The sedentary life, fatty diets and high body weights of our young modern females has removed the natural birth control of irregular ovulation know as adolescent subfertility. This is why our obese and out of shape girls can now get pregnant much younger, many having kids as young as age 13 today versus age 16 in 1900

But what about guys? What is a guy's natural contraceptive? Well, it's heat. Testicles remain outside his body (obviously the worse place to protect the family jewels) for one reason — they are thermal sensitive. They need to be cooler than then his body, because if they were kept at body temperature his sperm production would fail completely. When his balls get warmer, sperm count goes down. This is why bakers, welders and furnace workers all have low sperm counts, as well as taxi-drivers and white-collar desk workers who spend all day sitting. This is also true for guys who wear sexy thong underwear, which keep their balls shoved up against   their   body.

Oh, yeah. Another birth control device guys use:

They wage war.

DATING TOOLKIT #7: Is He Mr. Right for the Long Term? – Mammalian Selection Methods

Understanding how to captivate him and avoid the dangers of seduction eventually leads you to the final decision – is he the right one? He may have the success characteristics you seek, but does he have the genetic fit for your biology? Fortunately, nature gives you the tools to figure this out. Understanding them helps you choose Mr. Right more effectively.

Because the scientific evidence in this section may be inappropriate for younger readers or adults who are uncomfortable with discussing explicit sexual activity, it has been removed and the research data made available on our website:

www.sraleadership.com/DrPatAllen

If you are interested, this article reviews recent scientific determinations of genetic-fit between dating partners using mammalian methods involving sweat, kissing, and oral sex. Some of the elements discussed include biological, genetic revelations behind the following historical events:

- Napoleon's note to Josephine "I will be arriving in Paris tomorrow evening. Don't wash."

- In Shakespeare's day, why a girl kept a slice of apple under her armpits during dances and then gave it to the guy of their choice at the end of the evening so he could inhale this "love apple."

- In 1572, why Henry III of France inadvertently left his sweat- stained hanky in the cloakroom at the Louvre, the beautiful young Mary of Cleve found it and from that moment she conceived for him "the most violent passion."

- In Greece and the Balkans, why men carry handkerchiefs under their armpits during festivals and offer them to the women they invite to dance (they swear by the results).

• Why 19th century French novelist Joris Karl Huysmans followed women through fields to smell them, later writing that the scent from their underarms "easily uncaged the animal in man."

Conclusion

We're not extinct...yet. But until then, you now know the genetic secrets for getting a guy to date you. Despite all the differences between our genders, we like the philosophy of Richard Dawkins:

> **Let us try to teach generosity and altruism, because we are born selfish. Let us understand what our own selfish genes are up to, because we may then at least have the chance to upset their designs, something that no other species has ever aspired to...we, alone on earth, can rebel against the tyranny of the selfish replicators.**[87]

And rebel we can! Our behavior is not inevitably controlled by our genetic influences; nor can we just paint over our biology with new cultural meanings. Monogamy or infidelity, violence or tranquility, jealousy or indifference...men are not doomed to uncontrollable lust for multiple mates, and women are not doomed to scoff at men for feeling that way. On the other hand, new discoveries in genetics and evolution can help us understand why these sexual tensions occur and make more civilized choices, rather than simply comply with those delegated to us by evolution.

Fortunately, many of these choices are already available: birth control, fertility drugs, cyber-sex, video dating, sperm banks, test-tube babies, breast implants, tummy tucks and soon, human cloning. Dr. Helen Fisher said it best:

> **Our contemporary marriage patterns are a testament to the triumph of culture and personality over natural human tendencies... Just about every reproductive strategy known — except random promiscuity — is practiced by someone, somewhere. Some of us even choose celibacy or childlessness — genetic death. So malleable an animal is man.**[88]

These new choices offer us unparalleled possibilities to revolutionize ourselves. Our species has now developed new control over our mating behaviors, the proportion of which has been unprecedented in human evolution. Never before, in three and a half billion years, has any species on earth sought to understand its genetic program, or seek to upset it, to rebel against its selfish replicating genes.

**Remain unconscious of our genetic program
and risk following our species' million-year-old course. Wake up to this
program and find the power to override and even alter our evolutionary
trajectory.**

We see this impact today. Never before have we had the choice to "choose" our family. Now we can. We are no longer fated to be with our blood-family, and many have abandoned the Waltons' design of our forefathers. Divorce rates and successful single moms and dads are the result of different choices. If the kids spend holidays with non-bloods and we party with friends instead of family, so be it. Some of us now even choose to live alone or childless, or to relate on the internet instead of face-to-face — an electronics surrogate for physical communication and relationships. We now or very soon will have the power to alter marriage, genetics, parenthood, aging, and even death.

Ultimately, romance and lust are not accidents, but specific designs to encourage replication of genetic material. Which brings us to an important point:

**Even though we will continue to mate,
let's make sure we do it without harming civilization,
our partners, or ourselves.**

The choice is ours. Let's leave our children good ground to grow upon, and make our time with each other worthwhile. Let us:

- Be fruitful.
- Be kind.
- Be loved.

And never fight the fights none of us ever wanted to fight anyway.

ABOUT THE AUTHORS

Dr. Pat Allen

Dr. Pat Allen is a Marriage and Family Therapist (MFT), Certified Addictions Specialist, and Cognitive Behavior Therapist. She is also the Founder of the WANT® Institute, "Educators of Effective Communication Strategies" based on Transactional Analysis, and a woman who doesn't care at all about your feelings. She cautions that "Feelings, or your Pain, is just an indicator of change needed, or change in progress." Often called "The Love Doctor," she has a worldwide reputation for being politically incorrect — but scientifically accurate.

Dr. Pat's been a guest on hundreds of radio and television shows, including four appearances on Oprah, and is author of the best-selling woman's survival manuals Getting To "I Do" and Staying Married and Loving It. Rev. Michael Beckwith from the movie The Secret recognizes Dr. Allen as "a rare gift for our society," and relationship experts Marianne Williamson and Dr. John Grey credit her as an enriching influence in their own lives.

Dr Pat Allen has the answer to the question: How can men and women learn to successfully relate in this new millennium of confusing sexual roles, cyber-dating and demands for crippling political correctness? By studying how male and female energies interact, she has established clear and concise techniques that either sex can use to achieve greater intimacy in any relationship. This goes for anyone: straight, gay, or lesbian. Her patented technique of Androgynous Semantic Realignment has helped thousands of women to escape from unsatisfying relationships and finally make it to the altar through her books, workshops, and her weekly audience-participation show on male-female relationships that she's hosted in Los Angeles for the past 34 years — yes, that's every week for 34 years!

Do you feel he's just not that into you? Dr. Pat Allen will show you how to stop doing a Slam Dance with your significant other, and start doing a Romantic Waltz! For more information on Dr. Pat Allen's books, CDs, DVDs, workshops and seminars, visit www.DrPatAllen.com or call 310-390-4767.

Don Schmincke

Don began his career as a scientist and engineer, but after graduating from MIT and Johns Hopkins University he became fascinated with how people perform in groups (leadership-wise, that is, not sexually). Studying anthropology and evolutionary genetics, he ultimately discovered that most management theories fail because they don't take into account basic biological factors. The scientist in him prompted him into a new career: challenging conventional management theory and innovating ways to make the human machine more robust and successful.

Since then, Don's work in guiding executive leadership has been recognized by the American Management Association, as well as CNN, The Wall Street Journal, USA Today, Industry Week and over 60 industry publications. In addition, he's appeared on hundreds of radio and television programs worldwide, while his "Schmincke Research Alliance" (a nonprofit education center) workshops advance thousands of CEOs and executives every year towards extraordinary results by awakening exceptional leadership using timeless methods and ancient wisdom.

His irreverent humor and unconventional methods make him a refreshing change to common, status-quo management experts, and have established him as a consultant renegade and top speaker for the world's largest CEO member organization. Don lives in Baltimore, where he's on the faculty of Johns Hopkins and has enjoyed inflicting his unconventional techniques on innocent graduate students.

Among his top-selling management leadership books are High Altitude Leadership: What the World's Most Forbidding Peaks Teach Us About Success and The Code of the Executive: Forty-seven Ancient Samurai Principles Essential for Twenty-first Century Leadership Success.

Learn more about his unique approaches to management excellence at www.SRAleadership.com

APPENDIX
SCIENTIFIC RESEARCH FOOTNOTES

The Science Behind The Book

INTRODUCTION

1 Napoleon Hill, Think And Grow Rich, originally published in 1937.

CHAPTER 1

2 Research of Dr. Eric Vilain, Professor of Human Genetics, Pediatrics and
Urology as published Oct. 2003 in the Journal of Molecular Brain Research.

3 Research by Dr. Nancy Forger, Psychologist at the University of Massachusetts at Amherst.

4 Buss, David M. (2000), Dangerous Passion: Why Jealousy Is As Necessary As Love and Sex. New York: The Free Press, p.224.

5 Based on Nov. 4, 2003 issue of the American Heart Association journal Circulation and the work of Dr. Nieca Goldberg, cardiologist at Lenox Hill Hospital in New York, as reported 11/4/03 in the New York Daily News.

6 Based on a University of California at Berkeley study of lesbians from interviews of 720 adults at street festivals in San Francisco, published in the journal Nature, March/April 2000.

7 From research quoted by Dr. Margaret McCarthy, a physiologist at the University of Maryland School of Medicine at Baltimore, reported by the Associated Press.

8 I'd love to find out who started this internet list that hit the email circuit. Very creative.

9 Pease, Barbara and Allen (1998), Why Men Don't Listen and Women Can't Read Maps: How We're Different and What To Do About It. New York: Broadway Books, p.149; and Benderly, B.L. (1987), The Myth of Two Minds: What Gender Means and Doesn't Mean. New York: Doubleday.

10 McGuiness, D. (1976), Sensory Biases in Cognitive Development. Male-Female
Differentiation: A Bio-Cultural Perspective. New York: Praeger.

11 Kimua, D. (1989), "How sex hormones boost or cut intellectual ability," Psychology Today, Nov., pp.63-66; plus Weiss, R.S., "Women's skills linked to estrogen levels," Science News 134:341.

12 Benbow, C.P. and L.C. Stanley (1980), "Sex differences in mathematical ability: facts or artifact?" Science 210:1234-36, and (1983), "Sex differences in mathematical reasoning ability: more facts," Science 222:1029-31.

13 Leder, G.C. (1990), Gender Differences in Mathematics: An Overview. Mathematics and Gender. New York: Aldine.

14 Michael Gurian, What Could He Be Thinking? How a Man's Mind Really Works.

15 Often noted by Dr. Howard Gardner, Professor of Cognition and Education at Harvard University and author of Leading Minds: An Anatomy of Leadership.

CHAPTER 2

16 Joann Ellison Rodgers as she wrote in her book Sex: A Natural History. Henry
Holt, 2001.

17 Margulis, Lynn, and Dorion Sagan (2002), Acquiring Genomes: A Theory of the
Origins of Species. New York: Basic Books, Inc., p.52.

18 As reported in Fast Company magazine, Feb. 2003, p.100.

19 "Why Productive Fades With Age: The Crime-Genius Connection." Study published in 2003 in the Journal of Research in Personality that examined the lives of scientists, painters, jazz musicians, authors and criminals.

20 Pease (1998), op. cit. Pease's research references an American study bearing this out, p.161.

21 Gilligan, Carol (1982), In a Different Voice: Psychological Theory and Women's
Development. Cambridge: Harvard University Press.

22 Rodgers, Joann Ellison (2002), Sex: A Natural History, New York: Times Books
(Henry Holt), p.xv.

23 Crenshaw, Theresa L. (1996), The Alchemy of Love and Lust: How Our Sex
Hormones Influence Our Relationships. New York: G.P. Putnam's Sons, p.169.

24 Ibid.

25 Haselton, Martie G., and David M. Buss (2000). "Error management theory: A new perspective on biases in cross-sex mind reading," Journal of Personality and Social Psychology 78:81–91. Reprinted in Kenrick, D.T. (Ed.), (2004).
The functional Mind: Readings in Evolutionary Psychology. Needham Heights,
MA: Allyn & Bacon

26 Remember that study the Pease's referenced.

CHAPTER 3

27 Barash, David, and Judith Eve Lipton (2001), The Myth of Monogamy: Fidelity and Infidelity in Animals and People. New York: Henry Holt and Company, LLC, p.64.

28 Viet, O.G. (1982), "Gorilla society," Natural History, March p.45-58.

29 Fisher, Helen E. (1992), Anatomy of Love: The Mysteries of Mating, Marriage and
Why We Stray. United States: Ballantine Books, p.251.

30 "Mother and child disunion," Science News 3/20/04 on the research of Arthur Wolf, Stanford University Anthropologist and chronicled in Current Anthropology, Dec. 2003.

31 Fisher, op. cit. p.48.

CHAPTER 4

32 Ellis, B.J. and Symons, D. (1990), "Sex differences in fantasy: an evolutionary psychological approach," Journal of Sex Research, 27:527–556.

33 Buss (2000), op. cit. p.139.

34 Kenrick, Douglas, Sara E. Gutierres, and Laurie L. Goldberg (1989), "Influence of popular erotica on judgments of strangers and mates," Journal of Experimental Social Psychology, 25:159–67.

35 "Miller Lite's 'Catfight' ad angers some viewers," by Michael McCarthy, USA Today 1/14/2003.

36 Buddha, The Connected Discourses of the Buddha.

37 "But do girls want to be fancied by men behaving sadly?" by Melanie
McDonagh, Evening Standard, Nov. 24, 1998.

38 Low, Bobbi S. (2000), Why Sex Matters: A Darwinian Look at Human Behavior,
New Jersey: Princeton University Press, p.85–86.

39 Wright, Robert (1994), The Moral Animal: The New Science of Evolutionary
Psychology, New York: Vintage Books, p.70.

CHAPTER 5

40 Fisher (1992), op. cit. p.26.

41 Ibid. p.20.

42 Another fun item from the flurry of emails I got. Wish I knew who wrote it. Brilliant.

43 Hall, E.T. (1996), The Hidden Dimension. New York, Anchor Books.

44 Fisher (1992), op. cit. p.39.

CHAPTER 6

45 Buss, David (1994), The Evolution of Desire: Strategies of Human Mating, New
York: BasicBooks.

46 Wright (1994), op. cit. p.64.

47 Barash (2001), op. cit. p.54.

48 Research from a team of Scottish and Japanese researchers as reported in the journal Nature in June, 1999.

49 "Men and women, sex and Darwin," by Natalie Angier, New York Times
Magazine 2/21/1999; in the article she refers to David Buss' research.

50 Barash, David and Judith Eve Lipton (2001), The Myth of Monogamy: Fidelity and Infidelity in Animals and People. New York: Henry Holt and Company, LLC, p. 92.

51 Buss, David (1994), The Evolution of Desire: Strategies of Human Mating. New

York: Basic Books, p. 85.

52 The handicap theory is explained in "Mate selection—a selection for a handicap," Journal of Theoretical Biology 53:205-214 (1975) and "The cost of honesty" 67:603-605.

53 Barash (2001), op. cit. p.76.

54 Ibid. p.50.

55 Research of David Blanchflower of Dartmouth College and Andrew Oswald of Warwick University in Great Britain as published by the National Bureau of Economic Research and based on a University of Chicago database of a survey from 1988 to 2002 of 16,000 Americans.

56 Sommers, Christina Hoff (2000), The War Against Boys: How Misguided
Feminism Is Harming Our Young Men. New York: Simon & Schuster.

57 Crenshaw (1996), op. cit. p.166.

58 Buss, David (1994), The Evolution of Desire: Strategies of Human Mating. New
York: Basic Books, chapter 5.

59 From a 1991 study at the University of Engee in Turkey.

60 Fisher (1992), op. cit. p.163.

61 Based on study by neuroscientist Lucy Brown and colleagues at Stony Brook and Rutgers Universities, as well as British studies as mentioned in the Toronto Star, 2/14/03 in the article "Love arises in the unconscious."

62 Research of neurobiologists Andreas Bartels and Semir Zeki of University
College London in analyzing brain scans of people in love.

63 From the research of Helen Fisher, anthropologist at Rutgers University, as reported in the journal Neuroendocrinology, Dec. 2002.

64 Shostak, M. (1981), Nisa: The Life and Words of a !Kung Woman. New York, Random House.

65 Jankowiak, W.R. and E.F. Fischer (1992), "A cross-cultural perspective on romantic love," Ethnology 31 (no.2):149–55.

66 Janov, Arthur (2000), The Biology of Love. New York: Prometheus Books, p.292.

67 Crenshaw (1996), op. cit. p.4.

68 C. Sue Carter is Distinguished University Professor in the Department of Biology at the University of Maryland and is a guest researcher at the National Institutes of Health. She is widely recognized for her research in the hormone mechanisms that determine monogamous behavior in mammals.

69 Janov (2000), op. cit. p.300.

70 As reported by Susan Perry, primatologist at the Max Planck Institute for Evolutionary Anthropology in Leipzig, Germany in Science News, 4/3/04, vol.165.

71 From their book Why Men Don't Listen and Women Can't Read Maps.

72 Fisher (1992), op. cit. p.54.

CHAPTER 7

73 Watson, Lyall (2000), Jacobson's Organ and the Remarkable Nature of Smell. New
York: Penguin Putnam, Inc, 87.

74 The research is described very well in a book of the same name by Lyall Watson. Neurogeneticists have actually isolated the human gene that encodes for a pheromone receptor in the mucous lining of the nose, connecting it to the functionality of the VNO receptor, and call it V1RL1.

75 As reported in the March Proceedings of the National Academy of Sciences of research by Liman and Innan as well as research by Jianzhi Zhang and David Webb of the University of Michigan Ann Arbor.

76 Researcher Martha McClintock, as presented to an annual meeting of the
American Psychological Association.

77 Watson (2000), op. cit. p.87.

78 Reported in Nature Genetics, Feb., 2002, on the research of Dr. Carole Ober and Dr. Martha K. McClintock.

79 Watson (2000), op. cit. p.106.

80 Ibid. p.110.

CHAPTER 8

81 Dawkins, Richard (1989), The Selfish Gene. Oxford: Oxford University Press, p.111.

82 Research according to the Pew Research Center for People and the Press based on 38,000 interviews in 44 countries. Nicole Speulda, Project Director.

83 "World population to level off," reported 12/9/2003 in USA Today.

84 Dawkins (1989), op cit. p.111.

85 Baker, Robin (2000), Sex in the Future: The Reproductive Revolution and How It
Will Change Us. New York: Arcade Publishing, Inc., p.171.

86 Ibid. p.184.

CHAPTER 10

87 Dawkins (1989), op. cit. pp.3,201.

88 Fisher (1992), op. cit. p.161.

---

[i] Research of Dr. Eric Vilain, professor of human genetics pediatrics and urology as published in the Journal of Molecular Brain Research,

[ii] Buss, David (2000), The Dangerous Passion: Why Jealousy is as Necessary as Love and Sex, New York: The Free Press, p 224.

[iii] Based on Nov 4, 2003 issue of *Circulation* and the work of Dr. B.Nieca Goldberg, cardiologist at Lenox Hill Hospital in New York as reported in Daily News 11/4/03.

[iv] Based on a University of California at Berkeley study of lesbians published in March/April 2000 in the journal *Nature* from interviews of 720 adults at street festivals in San Francisco.

[v] I'd love to find out who started this internet list that hit the email circuit. Very creative.

[vi] From research quoted by Dr. Margaret McCarthy, a physiologist at the University of Maryland School of Medicine at Baltimore, in the Associated Press.

Made in the USA
San Bernardino, CA
27 April 2019